Your New Relationship With Money

*Mastering Money, Growing Wealth, and Finding
Freedom in a Culture Trying to Make You Broke*

Michael O'Leary

© 2019 Michael O'Leary

All rights reserved. No portion of this book may be reproduced in any form without permission from the author, except as permitted by U.S. copyright law.

Cover by Michael O'Leary

Book ISBN: 9781688547049

To my daughters,

Emma and Mia

Contents

Part 1: Time to Start Over With Money   1

1. The purpose of money and life   2
2. Dispelling the myths and misinterpretations   6
3. Reframe your concept of wealth   9
4. There's no standard path. It's not easy to find nor stay on.   12
5. Understanding your relationship with money   16

Part 2: Finding Your Purpose and Inspiration   23

6. A vision and purpose for money   24
7. Pick and pursue your priorities   27
8. Measure the right thing   33
9. The puzzle of employment and purpose   37
10. The things that slow you down   41
11. Lifestyle inflation is terrifying   45
12. Everything is a trap. A way to separate you from your money.   51
13. The ever-expanding desire for convenience   54
14. Understand how you spend money   59
15. Discover your inner DIY   63

Part 3: Understanding the Tools You'll Need   69

16. Compounding growth rates   70
17. Learning Excel and basic math   74
18. The most important tool there is   79
19. Keep track of your spending   85

20.	The dangers and opportunities of mortgages	90
21.	HGTV is distorting your reality	99
22.	Relax, it's just taxes	103
23.	Traditional retirement savings plans	109
24.	Credit and large purchases	115
25.	Don't hide cash under your mattress	118
26.	The art of negotiating	121
27.	Investing for growth	125

Part 4: Putting It Into Action — **131**

28.	You can do this	132
29.	Your net worth chart	135
30.	Net worth goal setting	140
31.	Tracking expenses and analysis	145
32.	Spending priorities and passions	149
33.	Throw out your budgets	153
34.	Benefits at work	159
35.	Retention departments and switching	165
36.	Saving money vs. not spending money	169
37.	Divvying up your paycheck	174
38.	Start investing yesterday	180
39.	Annual lifestyle deflation	184
40.	Financial independence	187

Your New Relationship With Money — **195**

Disclaimer

This book is about learning how to make your own decisions, not to make them for you. When it comes to money, no two lives are the same; what works for one person might not work for everyone. So please use this book to learn and make the best decisions for your life and circumstances.

The information provided in this book is for informational purposes only. It should not be considered legal or financial advice. You should consult with a professional to determine what may be best for your individual needs.

The author does not make any guarantee or other promise as to any results that may be obtained from using this content. No one should make any investment decision without first consulting his or her own financial advisor or conducting his or her own research and due diligence. To the maximum extent permitted by law, the author disclaims any and all liability in the event any information, commentary, analysis, opinions, advice and/or recommendations prove to be inaccurate, incomplete or unreliable or result in any investment or other losses.

Your New Relationship With Money

*Mastering Money, Growing Wealth, and Finding
Freedom in a Culture Trying to Make You Broke*

Michael O'Leary

Acknowledgments

Underneath and between the words in this book are a lifetime of influences, experiences, friendships, and growth. There have been many people that have influenced me and in turn, this book. My parents were unsurprising, the most influential in the area of personal finance. But it wasn't just the specific technical lessons or the memorable conversations; it was the totality of the life they created for their family. It was traditional at face value, but dramatically unconventional beneath the surface. That upbringing led me to challenge a lot of convention in my life, to explore, to learn, and to, most importantly, plot my path. I guess deep down though; it's their work that led to this book.

Additionally, I'd like to thank a group of very supportive friends with their assistance in editing, providing feedback and being enthusiastic throughout: Nick Okoro, Liz Nixon, Lisa Wolenberg, Teague de la Plaine, Ben Talbot, Dhara Jones, and Maggie Tucker, I can't thank you all enough.

And thank you to my wife Britta for letting me disappear for many months to complete this book.

How This Book Works

Your relationship with money is deep-rooted and will be difficult to change. You may not want to change it or feel like you should. It may seem overwhelming or not worth the trouble. Regardless of how open you are to change, that journey will require many adjustments to your thinking and your skillset.

This book is split into four parts, each building off the one before and each necessary to create a new relationship with money. You'll first need to dispel some misinformation you've unknowingly held as true for so long. Next, you'll need to find your motivation to push through some challenging tasks. With a clean slate and newfound inspiration, you'll also need some new skills and knowledge to effectively navigate future decisions. In the fourth and final part of this book, we'll create an action plan together.

Most of the concepts in this book aren't unique unto themselves. Saving money, investing for the future, maximizing tax deductions, pursuing your passions—all well studied and very well communicated topics. But everyone has a different perspective, a diverse set of biases and financial means at their disposal. There are many excellent books and blogs, but this book is about what has worked for me and what I believe to be most effective. How it is presented, what I think to be the most important and how to achieve those goals best—that's my book. Like all advice, I hope you'll read this with an open mind, a critical eye, and an appetite for change.

Part 1
Time to Start Over With Money

1. The purpose of money and life

Money as a pursuit onto itself is pretty meaningless. On a scale of life's necessities, money is the most important thing you need after the basics of food to eat, air to breath, a family to love. Unless you are hunting and gathering in the wilderness, you *need* money. And lots of it. Money serves many different purposes for people aside from purchasing necessities. Purpose is where this book starts as it is the foundation for a healthy and sustainable financial life.

Finding purpose and meaning in life is not something to be solved in this book, but it's essential to make the distinction between having a purpose for money and having a purpose for life. Perhaps along this journey, you'll develop a framework for a more robust purpose in your life, but in the end, whatever that purpose may be, you'll need money to achieve it and maintain it. Your purpose might be to raise children, achieve fame in sports, or science, or the arts. You may want to be a titan of industry or a voice for the underprivileged. Maybe you just want to see the world. Those achievements and lifestyles are journeys unto themselves, requiring years and dedication.

In parallel to those paths, you must also be building your financial life and finding a purpose for money. If you want to become a CEO, then money's purpose is to buy education and skills, to allow you to take risks in business and to fail. That is the purpose of money in achieving *that* life purpose. If you want to help those in need, then the purpose of your money is to give it away and make someone's life better, or to give you the time, free from the 9-to-5 grind where you can personally help others. That is the purpose of your money then and the reason you'll need and then desire to make sacrifices and tough decisions to get there.

If your purpose in life is to raise a family, then your purpose in earning and investing and spending money will be to support those you love and to help them find and achieve their purpose. This book starts with purpose and ends with the steps needed to fulfill that purpose. In between, we'll discuss the tools and knowledge needed to make it happen.

Whatever your purpose is in life, whatever your goals and aspirations, you'll most likely need the time to realize it fully. A couple of hours after work, a few weeks a year, it won't be enough. In that way, the purpose of money, eventually, becomes time. As you go through life, the money will serve to facilitate different milestones and achievements. For the future CEO, once tuition is paid, and the diploma is in hand, money then serves a new purpose. For the parents who pay for early childcare and then send their kid to school, money has provided that opportunity but now is earmarked for different education and activities. As you go through life earning and growing your money, the purpose for that money is constantly changing. For many people, perhaps most people, the purpose of money will eventually become time. We know this as retirement, but that's not exactly what this book is about. The purpose of money will ultimately be the freedom never to need it again. That's called financial independence, and it's a purpose in life that should encompass everything else. It doesn't matter if you want to work until the day you die and will never need to live off savings, that's not the point. If your purpose in life is to earn a paycheck, so be it; but creating the environment where you don't *need* to earn it, should be the purpose of money for everyone.

As you think about the purpose money serves in your life, and how it changes, it is critical to understand that the end goal of being financially independent isn't a final step, something to start only when the others have been fulfilled. If your milestones look like this, with financial independence at the end, the challenge might be impossible:

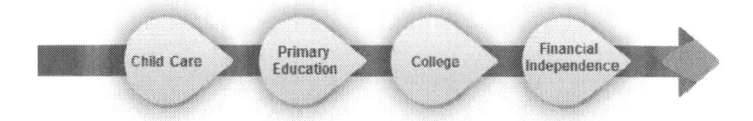

For a parent, money doesn't have a singular purpose of providing early childcare and then a unique purpose of primary education and then college, etc. There should be an underlying and interwoven purpose for your money. It is a flow chart like this.

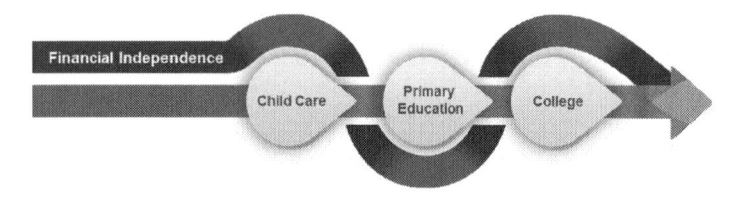

If your purpose is to raise a family, then you can't just focus on the immediate expenses of that goal. It must also be managed simultaneously with your overall purpose of financial independence. Because after you have raised your kids and provided for them, you will want the time to be with them.

The purpose you find for your life should be mirrored with a practical purpose for the money you earn. And no matter what your plans, you'll eventually need some level of financial independence and at the very least, financial security. But once you have a purpose for the money that transcends the constant noise of materialism and consumerism, you'll be working for something more significant than the next purchase and the next paycheck.

Remember This:

- *Whatever your purpose is in life, whatever your goals and aspirations, you'll most likely need the time to realize it fully.*
- *Creating an environment where you don't need to earn money should be the purpose of money for everyone.*
- *The journey of financial independence is a long-term pursuit of your life's purpose.*

2. Dispelling the myths and misinterpretations

Financial independence, wealth, retirement, high income, and other such aspirations are portrayed very specifically in American society. Especially when it comes to financial services, advertisers would have you believe that financial independence comes in one flavor:

- Retire at 65.
- Drive a nice car.
- Live in a beautiful beach house.
- Wear nice clothes.
- Not have a care in the world.

The underlying mythology is that the only future that you should aspire is the one marketers feed you. It's a harmful notion, resulting in a society that really can't see an option other than working your whole life, spending all your money. That's not a very compelling purpose, wouldn't you agree? The ironic part of this is that to achieve those things; you must earn and save an incredible amount of money only to blow through it in the remaining 5-15 years of your life. The system tells you to work your entire life, save a little bit of money, and then waste it on the things you deprived yourself of until that point. It's a heartbreaking notion to me, and it doesn't have to be the case.

With all of these forces working to create this imaginary lifestyle, separating you from your money, it's no surprise that people come up with reasons why they *can't* buck the trend and challenge the status quo. Let me know if you've heard these before or perhaps uttered them yourself:

- I want to enjoy my money
- I don't earn enough
- I need to earn more
- I enjoy working too much
- I'd be bored if I didn't work
- Kids are expensive
- I'm bad with money

By the end of this book and after a few months of lifestyle adjustments, you'll see right through these. Let me give you a quick debunking as to not distract you from the lessons in this book. A creeping of doubt can be pretty destructive on your journey.

- I want to enjoy my money: *Nobody enjoys money more than those who have a lot of it. Spend money wisely on your hobbies and passions and save the rest. That's how you enjoy it.*
- I don't earn enough/I need to earn more: *You probably just spend too much and don't invest what you do have.*
- I enjoy working too much: *If you didn't get paid, would you still work?*
- I'd be bored if I didn't work: *Explore the world, learn a new skill, and make new friends! You'll find your passion.*
- Kids are expensive: *True. That's not a myth. Having kids is a sacrifice at times, but sacrificing other expenses will solve this problem.*

Time to Start Over With Money

The modern economy is one of consumerism. Everyone and I mean everyone, needs you to spend money. Every brand, every company, every advertisement has a singular mission, and that's to separate you from your money. And they will tell you whatever you want to hear to make that happen. So ignore the myths and the stereotypes and standards. It only applies to you if you let it.

The other myth is that money is too hard to understand and manage yourself. Certified Financial this and that, Accredited so and so, Licensed yada yada; all titles that lead you to believe that understanding money is beyond your capabilities. The truth is that it's not a matter of training or education, but discipline. There are certainly some technical skills that you need to understand, but they don't require any formal degree or certification. I would even argue that it's easy to learn these concepts and skills. The only challenging part is the discipline needed to make it happen or to make a material change in your life.

So if you can see past the mythologies of retirement and financial independence, then all that stands in your way is the myth you tell yourself: *I'm bad with money.* Let's finish this book and see how you feel.

Remember This:

- *The system tells you to work your entire life, save a little bit of money, and then waste it on the things you deprived yourself of until that point.*
- *Set aside all the reasons you think you can't or don't want to change your relationship with money: they're all myths.*

3. Reframe your concept of wealth

Merriam-Webster defines wealth as "abundance of valuable material possessions or resources." But what is it to be "wealthy?" Wealthy in developed countries usually means luxury cars, large homes, lavish vacations, first-class travel, and 5-star meals, right? Your image of wealth might be slightly different, but it typically follows the same model. Perhaps it's a 15-foot boat or a 150-foot yacht. A 2,000 square foot house or a 20,000 square foot mansion. The problem is that this is the wrong way to characterize wealth. If you have $10 million, are you wealthy? What if you spend $9 million a year to be happy? Wealth should not be just a sum of assets, but more the value those assets bring to you for an extended time. The goal of everyone is to be happy and fulfilled in life, but sometimes that gets twisted into the pursuit of more and more.

I would challenge you to view wealth and your pursuit of wealth as the amount of time and happiness your money can buy you. Think of it as a ratio: assets divided by spending. The ultimate sign of wealth is when someone never needs to work or earn money. This level of abundance is going to be different for everyone, so what's yours? In the example above, I'd say that the person with $10 million who spends $9 million to be happy is not wealthy. The person with $10 million and spends $100,000 a year is insanely wealthy. And the person with $1 million who spends $50,000 a year and finds happiness is also wealthy. Even the person with $100,000 who spends $1,000 a year is wealthy. And the person who has nothing, but lives a self-sustaining life is wealthy. Where you live, how you live, what brings you satisfaction and fulfillment, these are all variables in the wealth calculation. This book is as much about growing your net worth as it is about lowering your spending and still being happy. This book is about becoming wealthy and the relationship you have with your income and your expenditure.

We look for measures and benchmarks to determine if we are wealthy, but wealth is a personal and private status. It's different for everyone, and there is only a loose correlation to the stuff you buy. Next time you say, "Wow, they must be wealthy." Or, "They come from a wealthy family," ask yourself how and why you are making that determination. Is it based on how happy they are and their level of financial resources relative to their baseline spending, or are you inferring wealth based on the things they buy and show you? It's easy to fake wealth, but it's hard to be satisfied. And it's really hard to be happy and financially independent if your goals of wealth are rooted in a consumerist ideal.

If you haven't found a lifestyle yet that makes you happy, I'd argue that perhaps you passed it a long time ago, but got so caught up in everything else that you didn't recognize it. You might not even need more money than you have right now if you can make your money go further. "Wealthy" might be closer than you think. But don't try to find "wealthy" in other people's lives. It won't be calculated for you in a magazine or online. Ignore everything that tells you how much you need or when you will retire. Only you can learn and know that, and it's different for every single person. Only you can see the level of spending that creates happiness in your life. This book is intended to help you create the most happiness possible.

Remember This:

- *If you have $10 million but need to spend $9 million a year to be happy, you're not wealthy.*
- *If you have $1 million and spend $50,000 a year to be happy, you're wealthier than that first guy.*
- *The ultimate sign of wealth is when someone never needs to work or earn money.*
- *Only you can determine if you're wealthy, so don't go looking for someone else's ideals.*

4.   There's no standard path. It's not easy to find nor stay on.

If you're reading this book, then you've already made a conscious decision to create a stronger financial future. Or perhaps you've identified a gap in your understanding of money or dissatisfaction with the status quo. The good news is that anyone can become financially independent and an expert with their money. But it's hard. Sometimes really hard. And it takes time. Definitely years. Likely decades. There's no standard path that everyone can follow to achieve financial independence or success. However, you may define it, the steps are always different, depending on your income, your location, your lifestyle, family size, hobbies, health, etc. What works for someone, might take years longer to achieve for another, or may not be possible at all. And in the end, everyone will have a different vision for their life and varied set of goals to achieve. Anyone who promises a few easy steps to achieve these goals is either mistaken or lying.

Now that I've told you that improving your financial life is confusing, complicated and time-consuming, let me share with you the upside: in addition to setting and achieve goals, the path toward financial independence becomes more accessible and more enjoyable over time. You won't be subjected to a 30-year struggle, full of misery, where at the end, the light comes on, and everything you ever wanted is suddenly achieved. You will learn and grow not just your money, but your understanding of money and your satisfaction in earning, saving, and spending it. Your relationship with these decisions and challenges becomes more transparent and more manageable over time. Like running, each mile you train gets a little bit easier, or you run it a little bit faster.

At its most basic level, everything in this book is a technique to increase the money you earn and reduce the money you spend. Someone who earns $1 million a year and spends only $20,000 is financially independent today, but that's not the reality for people. Most people spend everything they earn. And what's hard to see in these situations is that to spend that much money, people are both incurring new expenses and missing valuable opportunities. It's a painful cycle that keeps the poor, poor forever, and keeps the moderately well off working well into their 60s and 70s. As you go through this book, the concepts and techniques will seem easier or harder to implement compared to others. The primary driver of this disparity is your current level of income and your current level of spending. The more you spend, the more painful it will be to cut it back. And the less you earn, the less you'll be able to save considering that everyone has essential expenditures of food, housing, transportation, etc. that cannot be avoided.

The quadrant grid below illustrates the point. On opposite ends of the spectrum are high earners/low spenders and low earners/high spenders. In a later chapter, I'll explain the math behind these two types to show either how easy it can be to grow your wealth or how impossibly difficult it is respectively. Most readers, however, are going to fall into the medium-dark boxes, which present moderate difficulty in right-sizing their finances, but for different reasons. The high earners who are also top spenders will have to make dramatic lifestyle changes, which can be painful and challenging. The low earners who are low spenders won't need to make drastic changes to their lifestyle but will have to be extremely focused and effective in their earning and wealth-generating activities. Then they are many people somewhere in between.

	Low Spending	Medium Spending	High Spending
High Income	Easy	Easier	Moderately Difficult
Medium Income	Easier	Moderately Difficult	Very Difficult
Low Income	Moderately Difficult	Very Difficult	Impossible

If you're a lower earner and spending more than you earn, that's the most challenging position. And if you're a high earner, but a low spender, you need only a few tweaks to propel you down the path of financial growth.

We're going to work on both requirements for financial improvement though: reducing spending and growing your income. This financial journey isn't a decades-long grind, though. As your wealth growths, earning becomes easier and accumulates faster. The result of more significant income is that saving more and more over time becomes not just feasible, but comfortable. At some point, you'll be on cruise control, immune (or at least resistant) to spending impulses, smart with your management of money and laser-focused on what you need to do to achieve that vision for your life.

Whatever you do, though, don't rely on other people for the answers. I say that as I'm writing a book with "all the answers," but the distinction is that understanding *how* to make decisions and what to look for allows you to come to the conclusions that work for you. There will certainly be some overlap in the advice you consume, the rules that work for the many and also fit your specific situation, but you shouldn't take it a face value. Your life and circumstances will also change over time, and only when you understand money, the tools at your disposal and your vision, can you make the best, most effective decisions. This book is about finding a path that fits your life. And help you stay on it.

Remember This:

- *Promises of specific results based on general feedback are almost always wrong.*
- *The path of financial independence will be different for everyone. For some, it will be easy, for some almost impossible.*
- *Over time, the journey will become more manageable as results built and momentum grows.*

5. Understanding your relationship with money

Money as a pursuit onto itself is pretty meaningless. That's simply greed. To understand the role money plays in your life and to modify it, let's first look at Maslow's Hierarchy of Needs. For those of you unfamiliar with the Hierarchy, it's the brainchild of American psychologist Abraham Maslow. Published in 1943, it describes the five levels of "needs" that humans have. Each level, starting from the bottom, builds upon the one prior as needs are met in life. The first need is Physiological, otherwise known as food, water, shelter, etc. Then comes Safety, which is not only physical but can be financial or emotional safety as well. After those basic needs are met, people seek Love and Belonging found in family, community, and romance. Esteem is an interesting one as this level is about the desire for self-esteem, recognition, and attention. Lastly, there's Self-Actualization or fulfilling your potential. Maslow would argue that you must achieve each level before advancing or realizing the next.

Your New Relationship With Money

- Self-Actualization (1)
- Esteem (2)
- Love/Belonging (3)
- Safety (4)
- Physiological (5)

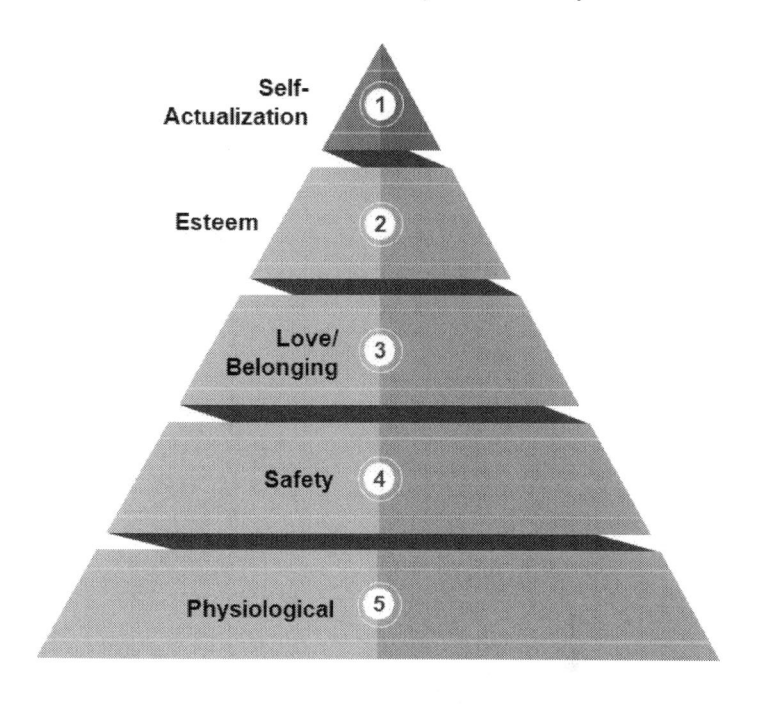

You can interpret this pyramid many ways, but if you're reading this, then consider that self-actualization part to be found in financial independence and the freedom you have to focus entirely on your purpose and passions. It's a state of existing free from the burden of an employer, unrestricted by the need to earn money and unleashed upon the world to be present with the people most important to you, explore the places that create a sense of adventure and dive deeply into the passions that satisfy and fulfill you.

If Mr. Maslow permits me, I'd like to modify this pyramid just a little. Let's call it the Hierarchy of Spending. As you can see, Love/Belonging and Esteem are no longer there.

```
        ┌─────────────┐
        │      /\     │
  Self- │     /1 \    │
Actualization /____\   │
        │   /      \   │
        │  / Safety 2\ │
        │ /_____\ │
        │/            \│
        │ Physiological 3│
        └─────────────┘
```

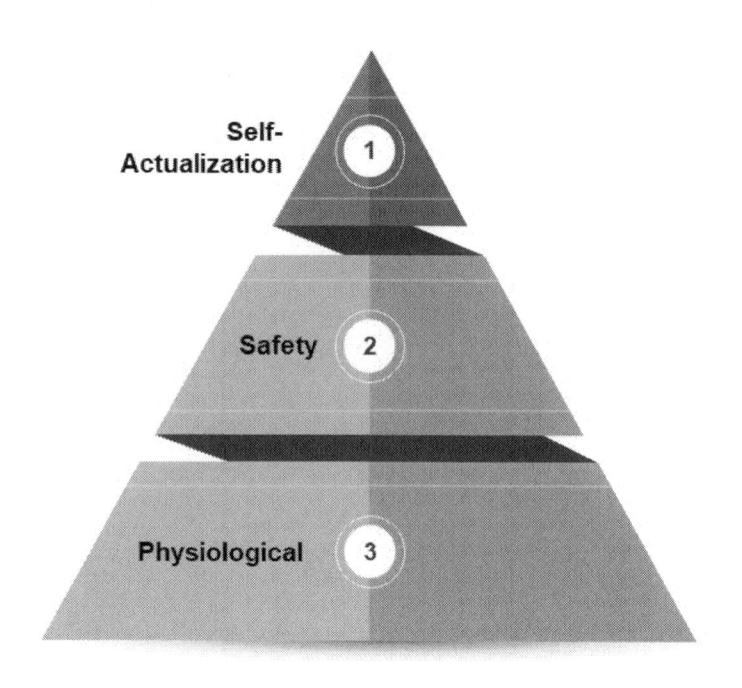

(Pyramid diagram: Self-Actualization (1) at top, Safety (2) in middle, Physiological (3) at bottom)

These three levels you can buy, the other two you cannot. Money can't buy friends or love; it can't buy self-esteem or self-worth. That isn't to say that *earning* money doesn't garner attention or prestige, because it certainly can. *Spending* money won't get you that, though. Spending money can create envy, but that's not what the Hierarchy of Needs is. Now the Hierarchy of Spending is what you can and should spend money to achieve. Quite obviously, money buys food and shelter, and it can purchase safety of different kinds. And having *enough* money can buy you financial independence and the opportunity for self-actualization. But if you leave the other levels in there, you'll most certainly delay the final level and perhaps never reach it. Trying to buy love and relationships and trying to spend your way into self-esteem is a dangerous and costly undertaking.

Practically speaking, this means that you should spend money on what creates a healthy and safe life. Spend money on the things that make you happy, but avoid the trappings of those expenses aimed at earning praise, envy, or admiration. Let your actions and attitudes do that. Instead, save and grow your money to reach the top of the pyramid. You'll not only have a lot of money, but you'll have friends and family who care about *you*, not what *you own*. And I would venture to guess that the energy you saved from a lifetime of anxious materialism has been directed and focused on some exciting and fulfilling endeavors.

A friend of mine commented many years ago that even when I retire and have the opportunity to enjoy my saved money, I will still pinch pennies, shop for bargains and never, ever splurge. It was a joking sort of conversation, but it did get me thinking: Will I ever *enjoy* my money?

The answer is yes, and no. The first thing that you have to understand is that people enjoy money differently. Some people enjoy spending it: the act of exchanging earned money for items or services gives some people a rush. I don't think it's unreasonable for me to say that this is a temporary enjoyment and serves as the root of most financial problems. For these people, enjoying money is about the things they can exchange for it.

For those people already engaged in this relationship between money and financial independence, money is about owning the direction of one's life. Saving money is enjoyable because having money saved up gives you the freedom to make decisions about your life. When you need money to live, your time isn't your own. Your time belongs to your employer and your incoming-generating activities. Time isn't just your time at work; this is your time figuratively as well. You must work and earn money to live your life. Everything else that's important in your life comes second and must balance around your income. Balance is excruciatingly stressful for many people, especially when money is tight.

When you have money and when you have no more need for income, your time becomes wholly your own. You probably think of this as retirement. You're probably not there yet, but the *pursuit* of it can also yield some of this freedom. You won't live paycheck to paycheck, feeling trapped in need to earn more money every two weeks. That freedom, although not absolute, will be enjoyable. You have control and power in your life when you have resources. Those feelings permeate other areas of your life, creating new confidence, inspiring some further risk-taking and adventure.

If this mindset seems farfetched or unrealistic, don't accept that to mean that it doesn't apply or you can't feel that way. It just doesn't apply *yet*. You've likely spent your entire life thinking only of the things money buys and how those things make you feel. Money by itself might feel meaningless to you, and that's ok. This book will hopefully help foster many dimensions of meaning for money and the role it plays in your life.

The relationship you have with money can either be about the "stuff" it buys you, or the freedom it affords you. Your relationship shouldn't be built on the answer to the question, "What can I buy with my money?" Start to ask yourself, "What can I achieve *because* of my money?"

Remember This:

- *Money can't buy love and self-esteem, but it can buy freedom for self-actualization.*
- *When you need money to live, your time isn't your own. It's your employers.*
- *When you have money and when you have no more need for income, your time becomes wholly your own.*

Time to Start Over With Money

Part 2
Finding Your Purpose and Inspiration

6. A vision and purpose for money

What is it that you want? It's a pretty basic question and one that most people would say they have an answer for, but not really. Let's go through a little exercise that I like to do with people who come to me for help:

>Me: "What is it you want to do with your life?"
>Them: "I'd like to keep working and then retire by 60."
>Me: "And then what will you do when you retire?"
>Them: "Oh, I don't know. Travel probably. Play a lot of golf."
>Me: "That's it?"
>Them: "I've always wanted to live somewhere else, so maybe I'd buy a home on the coast. I want to build a home. I've always wanted to do that."
>Me: "Ok, so why wait until you're 60."
>Them: "What do you mean?"
>Me: "Why not do all those things earlier in your life? Why not do them at 50? Or 45?"
>Them: (Pause)
>Them: How is that possible?

Every conversation is like this. Most people have resigned themselves to the idea that there is no other path except working their entire adult lives. 60 sounds like a good number. 70 is too close to your death and depresses you. It's less than 65, which you might read is normal. It's not in your 50s because that would be ridiculous. Right?

Your vision for your life is going to be unique, and I'm not going to instruct you on what your life should look like, what passions you should pursue, or what goals to achieve, but I will suggest that they will all require one thing: time. Even if your life's goal is to buy a 100-foot yacht and look at it, you'll want *time* to do that. In the business world, time is money. In your life, money is time.

I used to think that the childhood exercise of picking what you'd do "if you didn't need money" was a silly one. You need money I thought, and you can't make a living doing watercolors of butterflies or writing haikus (I am not disparaging either of these pursuits. They sound quite nice actually). The exercise, though, did hold some value as I later determined. What makes you the happiest? What brings you joy? Focus on that. Pursue that. And never, ever lose sight of that. The error in that childhood exercise is that the question was inherently narrow: do one thing that you love and do it for money.

But in most cases, it is painful and usually impossible to align your greatest passions with a paycheck. It's certainly worth a shot, but in most cases, life doesn't work out like that. Where this idealized exercise ends up leading people is to a belief that work must equal passion and enjoyment. You should, with great enthusiasm, try to turn your passion into a paycheck. But if it doesn't work out, don't tangle yourself into knots convincing yourself that what you do for a paycheck is your passion. When we look at Maslow's Hierarchy, your passion is the top level of Self-Actualization, and it might not be something you're aware of at this point in your life.

Most people reading this book will be early-to-mid-career, and I wouldn't recommend quitting your job to do watercolors of butterflies. If you couldn't turn your passion into a paycheck, make that passion the reason you earn money. If you haven't found your passion yet, make that quest for a passion, the reason you earn money. If you

Finding Your Purpose and Inspiration

can identify what you want most in life, then earning money and saving money becomes much more than a bi-weekly paycheck and a monthly credit card bill. There is a purpose behind the work you do and the money you earn. There is a reason to sacrifice on spending that perhaps wasn't there before.

There's a dilemma that you'll face once you buy into a new vision for your life and a purpose for your money: you can't have it both ways. You can't spend all your money and also free yourself from the burden of needing that paycheck.

How you go about developing your purpose for money and the vision you hope to achieve isn't my area of expertise, but I would encourage you to conduct the childhood exercise where you ask yourself what you'd do "if you didn't need money." If the answer is "video games", that's ok, but keep thinking. Continue down that path and identify what specifically brings you joy and satisfaction. How would you participate in that thing if you had money and also had time, a lot of time?

The vision for your life can be complex or basic. It can be specific or vague. It can involve achievement or a constant pursuit. Whatever that vision is, make money the vehicle that gets you there. And when you've aligned yourself to that mission, I think you'll find an endless source of inspiration to do all the seemingly mundane or boring or difficult tasks managing money requires.

Remember This:

- *In the business world, time is money. In your life, money is time.*
- *If you couldn't turn your passion into a paycheck, make that passion the reason you earn money.*
- *If you haven't found your passion yet, make that quest for a passion the reason you earn money.*

7. Pick and pursue your priorities

Let's say that you have determined your purpose to be raising a family and traveling the world. And the ultimate purpose of your money is achieving financial independence to do as much traveling with your family as you can. Every spending, saving, and investment decision you make is in support of this purpose, and you gain some clarity about what the trade-off is with every decision. But you can't save, save, save, and be miserable until the point you stop and focus solely on life's purpose. This is not an all or nothing game. How you manage your needs, your wants, and your long-term goals will help you find enjoyment and fulfillment on the entire journey, not just the end.

When searching for balance, it's essential to create your spending priorities. Otherwise known as the categories of spending that enrich your life, allow you to achieve your goals and make you feel good about spending. There's no point in having money if you don't spend it, I get that. It's important to spend it wisely and to spend it on the things that have the most substantial return on investment (ROI). Sometimes that ROI can't be tracked in a spreadsheet. Having money is to have the freedom to enjoy your life. Develop your core spending priorities!

Let's first talk about what core spending priorities are not:
- Expenses that are meant to elicit envy from others.
- Expenses that allow you to "fit in."
- Expenses that someone else tells you will make you happy.
- Expenses that attempt to fill an emotional void.

So what are core spending priorities? They are not things, but facets of your life that help you achieve happiness. Here are some common ones that most people would agree with:

Core Spending Priorities

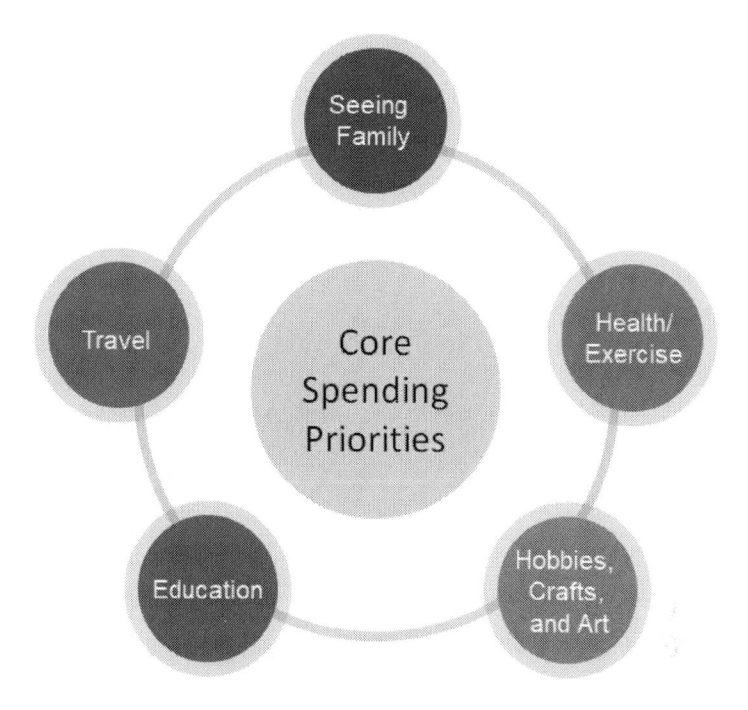

- Seeing Family
- Travel
- Health/Exercise
- Education
- Hobbies, Crafts, and Art

Let me give you an example of how this works: Having a core priority does not mean you spend freely. You still have to scrutinize everything, but the difference is that you feel good about it. You allow yourself the freedom to say, "I'm going to do this no matter what, now how do I do it wisely?" So let's take travel and family:

1. You want to see your parents in a different state over Christmas.
2. It's a priority to both travel and to see your family.
3. You will spend the money to travel there no matter what. The decision is automatically made to incur the costs necessary to make this trip. Mentally, you've accepted that even if it costs thousands of dollars per ticket, you'll still go.

Finding Your Purpose and Inspiration

But you don't buy a First Class ticket, or the first flight you see. You look for a deal, and if it's outrageously expensive to fly over Christmas, maybe you'll drive, or go the week before. No matter what, you go. And when you spend the money, you feel good about it. Perhaps you spent $1,000 to get there, which is a lot, but it's a priority, so it's worth it. You could have spent $2,000 or $3,000, but you worked hard to find the least expensive option, and you went with it.

$1,000 on clothes might give you a heart attack, but a $1,000, in this case, shouldn't make you sweat. It's imperative that spending is compartmentalized when it comes to regret and guilt. If you're not spending money on your long-term purpose or your priorities and passions, you're simply taking away from the things that truly matter the most. That's regrettable.

Wait for a second though; What if you don't have anything you'd list as a hobby? What if you haven't found your passions? That's ok. Hobbies, interests, and ultimately passions aren't built into your DNA, you must discover them. You might even have to practice and cultivate them before they provide the level of fulfillment you might expect. Everyone discovers their passions in different ways and over vastly different timelines. Whether you find your passions at age 6 or 60, what's important is that you let yourself find them. And most importantly, you must create an environment in your life where you can pursue them.

So when it comes to determining where to spend your money, give yourself the freedom to pursue many different things. Take art classes, volunteer with various groups, practice different crafts, read as much as you can.

You'll find something worth identifying as a priority for the rest of your life.

Having a core spending priority means that after you've done the research and found the most cost-effective way to make your purchase, you never feel bad about it. And feeling bad about these important purchases can be an obstacle when you build momentum toward fiscal discipline. So if travel brings you great joy, do the research, find the best flight, travel in Economy, stay in a reasonable hotel and have yourself an adventure; and never again question if it was worth the cost. But don't book a business class ticket for 5-times the price when an Economy ticket gets you to the same place.

Be careful with your boundaries, though. Where do your priorities end and materialism begin? The edges of these priority categories are blurred or non-existent for many people. The result is that all kinds of things are purchased with the same lack of scrutiny or indifference; both the categories that bring great joy to someone's life as well as those categories that bring only short-term entertainment value or no value at all.

The core spending priorities are the things that create the most value and most *sustained* happiness, the biggest bang for the buck. Don't get confused about how to treat your spending within these categories though; just because a category provides the most significant amount of happiness, it does not mean that you can be frivolous. If you save money in many areas of your life only to overspend it on your priority categories, you are still no closer to financial independence. If you set your priorities, scrutinize those expenses, and also cut back in the non-value-add areas as well, you can have both immediate

Finding Your Purpose and Inspiration

happiness and fulfillment and long-term realization of your purpose.

Remember This:

- *Core spending priorities are categories of spending that enrich your life, allow you to achieve your goals and make you feel good about spending.*

- *How you manage your needs, your wants, and your long-term goals will help you find enjoyment and fulfillment on the entire journey, not just the end.*

- *If you're not spending money on your long-term purpose or your priorities and passions, you're simply taking away from the things that truly matter the most.*

8. Measure the right thing

Ok, so enough with the philosophy. Let's get to the stuff with dollar signs. The most important concept in growing wealth is net worth. It is not your salary, your cash flow, your bonuses, the value of your house, etc. From here on out, every decision you make about money comes down to one question: how does this grow my net worth? This subject is so important that we'll discuss it in each of the next 3 Parts of this book. Becoming net worth-focused is crucial.

Net worth is the cash value of everything you have in liquid assets or assets you could sell, less any liabilities (debts). Your 401k counts. Your checking account counts. Your car. Your house. Your mother's pearls. Your stamp collection. All should be given a value and tallied in a chart. And in case you start going down this path: Your $500 shoes aren't worth $500, they are worth about $10, which is maybe what the government will return to you when you donate them. And let's not forget your liabilities! Credit cards, student loans, mortgages? All need to be on the chart. $10,000 in the bank and $10,000 in credit card debt equals $0 on the net worth chart.

So how does keeping this chart help you save money? Easy: does the total value of your assets grow every month? If the answer is yes, then okay, you are living within your means and saving money. Or does your net worth decline? Declines could be investment-related of course, but adjusted for broad, directional movements in the market; a drop means you are living outside your

Finding Your Purpose and Inspiration

means and spending more than you earn. That's pretty bad news.

We'll discuss later how to calculate your net worth, how to track and analyze it, and how to make decisions about your life based on it. For now, though, let's explore why this framework matters. There are numerous things you can do with your money, and each one comes with its unique expenses and opportunity costs. Let's say you earn $100:

1. What if you need that $100 before payday? You can go to a payday lender and go home with $50.
    ➢ You can invest that $50.
2. If you take the $100 in your normal paycheck, you pay taxes on it and go home with $75.
    ➢ You can invest that $75.
3. What if you don't take the money immediately, though? That's an option too.
    ➢ You can put the $100 into the company 401k and pay no taxes on it (at least now), and you get a 6% match, so $6. You now have $106 invested.

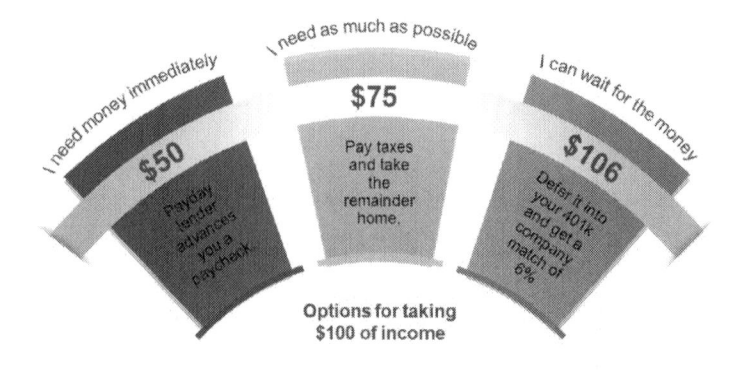

Options for taking $100 of income

- I need money immediately → **$50** — Payday lender advances you a paycheck
- I need as much as possible → **$75** — Pay taxes and take the remainder home.
- I can wait for the money → **$106** — Defer it into your 401k and get a company match of 6%

34

In all three scenarios, you earn $100, but your investable remainder can be $50, $75 or $106. Your mindset should be singularly focused: how do I maximize every dollar. The person who takes the $50 from the lender is prioritizing a very immediate need to spend it. The person who takes home the $75 in their paycheck is prioritizing steady cash flow to cover expenses. The person who postpones the earning of that money by putting it into a 401k now has significantly more. Each person has a priority, and the reasons for each might be compelling, but if you've aligned yourself to your purpose, there is only one choice: the one that creates the most value.

The big challenge people have in adopting a net worth focus is that most people believe cash flow is the key metric. If you are focusing on cash flow, you're probably paying for large purchases in installments, leasing cars, extending your 30-year mortgage another ten years, etc. If you *need* cash, you'll pay extra for that flexibility. If you don't need cash, you'll earn a return on it. All of the options for your money act like loans, if you are taking and spending more money, you're paying for that privilege. If you can get your finances to a point where you're not living paycheck to paycheck, suddenly the world opens up, and you can selectively allocate your money to the places that earn it the highest return.

The net worth view also gives you the cleanest and most dynamic approach to determining your plans. In the end, all the money is yours, and you can spend it. For periods of your life, it may be locked up though, and that can be difficult for people to accept. A contribution to a 401k is only available when you turn 59.5 (to avoid penalties), a principal payoff on your mortgage is only available again once you sell the house, a 529 college savings contribution can only be spent on a child's higher education. But all of these are your assets, and eventually, they'll all be turned into spendable cash.

So while it's difficult to "put money away," if you can get over the emotional hurdle of that detachment, your wealth will grow far faster than if you take the cash into your checking account. And that's what the net worth mentality does; it forces you to look at all your assets, regardless of their restrictions, as a single view. We'll get into the mechanics of creating a spreadsheet view of this later, but after a few months of tracking your net worth and watching it grow, that feeling of detachment from your money will go away.

It's hard to escape the great game of consumerism that is thrust upon us. To constantly need the newest and best, to out-purchase your neighbors and to never have enough. Taking a net worth view of your life changes the rules of the game and for those of you who still need the competitive edge, playing the net worth game is one you'll win more often than not. It's not how much you earn or how much you buy; it's how much you keep and how much you grow. $1 million in income, paired with $999,990 of expenses yields $10 of net worth (let's assume the spending was all frivolous). But $50,000 of income and $35,000 of expenses creates $15,000 of net worth. Spending $80,000 on a new car that's worth $70,000 the next day has created a net-negative result: you've spent $80,000 of cash in exchange for an asset worth only $70,000, a loss of $10,000. So don't worry about income, or spending, or the size of your house. Worry about your net worth. If you play by those rules, you'll end up a winner. Play by the rules of materialism, and you'll always end up losing out.

Remember This:

- *From here on out, every decision you make about money comes down to one question: how does this grow my net worth?*
- *If you need cash, you'll pay extra for that flexibility. If you don't need cash, you'll earn a return on it.*
- *It's not how much you earn or how much you buy; it's how much you keep and how much you grow.*
- **NET WORTH.**

9. The puzzle of employment and purpose

There are many great books about work, life, work/life balance, integration, and so on. I won't try to answer the question of how to achieve a balance of work and life, because it is different for everyone. It is different based on your job, your industry, your location, your age, your position in the organization. My feelings about the subject are mixed, and they've evolved as my life and career has changed. Employment is an extraordinary thing, as are careers and professions and skills, but not in the way you're probably thinking about it right now. The line between employment and purpose is often blurred.

Finding Your Purpose and Inspiration

Sometimes it's blurred because you've found a way to make your purpose in life the source for your income. That's incredibly rare, and I truly envy those people. But what happens when your employment ends? When purpose and a paycheck are the same, losing one means losing everything. That is a precarious position to put yourself.

For the majority of people whose purpose and passion is not the source of their paycheck, the line can start clearly defined and grow fuzzy over time. Because you need money to pursue your purpose, you need to work and earn money. Therefore it isn't a stretch to then, over time, believe that the source of your income is your purpose: it allows you to achieve the things you want in your life. Employment will enable you to do all the things in life that require money but don't mistake employment as your purpose if there is something greater you want to achieve.

It is ok to admit that your income-earning job isn't your passion. You can be enthusiastic about it and find enjoyment from it, but if your life's purpose lies outside employment and if your passions are located elsewhere, embrace it.

Employment doesn't always align with your values in life. Lofty values like compassion, spirituality, honesty, love, or service are all things that are hard to align in a professional world. Businesses aren't usually *opposed* to these values, and many people within those companies will identify with and share those personal values, but the businesses themselves almost always will operate outside them. And in many cases, the business might operate in direct conflict with the values that are important to you.

Only when there is an economic incentive to be honest or compassionate will a company be so. To be fair, there are some business leaders who put their personal values ahead of their company's economic performance, but this is rare. In most cases, a company committing to reducing waste, donating to needy causes or embracing social benefits like paid maternity leave, are done to leverage an economic advantage. The positive press, engagement with the local business community or the retention of employees all have economic benefits, and that's why companies do them. Again, to be fair, these actions might genuinely align with the personal beliefs of the leaders making those decisions, but companies exist to create profit.

Don't get me wrong, I'm not averse or opposed to work, careers, trades and the like. Work is a critical part of life, and it's what all societies, albeit in different ways, develop young people to do eventually. Education at all levels is building towards creating a functional and contributing member of society and the economy. If you don't pursue a career and work for a substantial amount of time, you are missing out on the formative experience. The skills, expertise, and social skills, to name a few, are invaluable and will help you have a more fulfilling life. So let's be clear here: you need to work hard in your life and create a meaningful resume of experiences, skills, and relationships. Learn to negotiate the world, interact with a variety of personalities, and solve problems. Those things transcend employment.

And of course, you need the money. None of what we're discussing in this book can be accomplished without money. The more money you make, the easier it will be to save it and then pursue whatever life you want. Some people are lucky enough to have found a passion and get paid for it. But most don't have that. But just because work isn't your passion doesn't mean that you shouldn't pursue every avenue for success in your career. You'll make some sacrifices over time, and it will be worth it until it's not worth it.

If you can find your purpose, work is a means to an end. When work begins to interfere with your purpose and passions, including your family, it's not worth the sacrifice. When work is what makes you unhappy and prevents you from being a good friend, or parent or family member, it's not worth it. Your employment will, at some point in life, cross the threshold where it does more harm than good. You must be prepared for that point financially. And if you have built a strong career and resume, you can find new employment if that's what you want. Or you can quit entirely.

Some people are very fortunate to have found their purpose and turned it into a paycheck, but for everyone else, don't let the need for a paycheck become your reason for being. When you die, no one will care what you did for a paycheck. They'll care about how you treated them, how much time you spent with them. Your relationship with money is also about your relationship with people along the way.

Remember This:

- *Employment will enable you to do all the things in life that require money but don't mistake employment as your purpose if there is something greater you want to achieve.*
- *You need to work hard in your life and create a meaningful resume of experiences, skills, and relationships.*
- *You'll make some sacrifices over time, and it will be worth it until it's not worth it. You must be prepared for that point financially.*

10. The things that slow you down

Saving money and growing wealth is a lot like a race car starting at zero: it takes a tremendous amount of power to get off the line and to reach top speeds, the driver must expertly change gears until the top speed is reached. But once you reach that top gear, you're going. Take your foot off the pedal for a second, and you're still cruising at top speed. It's getting up to that point that taxes both the driver and the car. To get up to cruising speed, you'll need to work hard. And there are no shortages of things to slow you down. The track is strewn with obstacles and debris placed there deliberately by others.

Getting involved in your finances and making tough or complicated decisions is where many people fail; they fail even to get started in any meaningful way. But it's also not enough to decide to let someone else do it for it. There is an infinite number of financial advisers and planners and websites around, and while that is a significant first step, it's not good enough. Generally speaking, all of these voices tell you what you want to hear, make it seem more complex or less complex than it really is, and put you in the passenger seat of your own life. You won't get there very fast if you don't take an active role. If you do decide to be proactive and take charge, being timid, indecisive, or risk-averse will also slow you down. If you get a piece of financial advice that seems pretty doable, not-so-hard, riskless, and so on, it's not going to generate the types of results you want.

All of these personal aversions to taking control of your financial planning pale in comparison to the devastating effects of spending. While the most crucial step you must first take towards financial independence is the creation of a vision for your life, a close second is overcoming the grip marketers have over you and their power to manipulate you into buying things. No one cares about your stuff, and you shouldn't care about theirs. Let me repeat that for effect: no one cares about your stuff. They're too busy thinking about themselves. It is a most vicious and ever-expanding spiral of spending that most people find themselves locked into forever. As a kid, you wanted a $10 toy to impress your friends. As a teenager, it was a $100 jacket. As a young professional, it's a $1,000 watch. It gets much more harmful after this: $100,000 cars and $1,000,000 homes.

Of course, you can argue that these are the only items that bring you pleasure and joy and fulfillment in life, and maybe that's true. Probably not, but let's say for a minute that it is true: You are genuinely happy in your $1,000,000 home. You could also be happy somewhere else, and most likely, a big part of your decision-making to purchase that home in the first place came from wanting to appear successful to others. Could you be happy in an $800,000 house? A $500,000 house?

People are too busy worrying about themselves to appreciate and envy your possessions. Luxury cars, expensive homes, 5-star hotels, and First Class flights, and the outsourcing of every minor task in your life won't just slow you down; they'll ruin you. And in the end, nobody cares what car you drive. They may look at it enviously, or even comment on it, but they won't care the next day. People are too busy worrying about themselves to genuinely care about what you own. They see your car and think about the car they want, how they'd pay for it, how you'd feel about them if they drove it, how they'd feel about themselves. They don't care about you and your stuff; they care about themselves. So why bother with any of it?

These are some of the biggest pitfalls and spending traps people get themselves sucked into, but an overarching problem that compounds these pitfalls and also exists as a problem unto itself is borrowing money. If it's a mistake to buy an $80,000 car, it's an absolute travesty to finance or lease it. Purchasing a $1,000,000 home might be a stretch, but borrowing $900,000 to do it can slow your financial growth to a crawl. And let's not even get into credit card debt, which can be the most expensive debt there is.

Finding Your Purpose and Inspiration

The bottom line is that overspending is a big problem, one that, at the very least, slows down your journey towards financial independence, and at worst, completely derails it. If you are also borrowing money and paying interest (financing) or paying for the privilege of borrowing an item (leasing), you'll make the problem even worse. The good news is that both issues can be solved simultaneously when you begin to prioritize your spending and give up the large or luxury or social status spending. You won't need to borrow money because you aren't spending it.

Depending on when in your life you start this journey, charting a new direction, the going may be slow. This pace can be an enemy onto itself and discourage you from continuing. You might only be able to save $100 at first, and that might only buy one share of a particular stock, and after a year, you might only have $103 from that original investment. The insignificance of this new $3 would likely cause you to question the whole purpose. Why not just wait until you're earning a little more or when you no longer have student loans. This logic might be the most detrimental of them all. But just because you can't save a material amount of money *now* or your return on investment isn't a jackpot *now*, you can't give up, and you can't slow down.

Whether or not you face this conflict of expectations depends mostly on where you are in your life and your lifestyle. The more you currently spend, the more money you will need to "see" for it to be material in value. Going back to the earlier examples, if you're a kid and you save $10, that's a huge accomplishment. But if you're 50, that number will likely need to be $10,000 to have the same effect. Regardless of what amount of money seems real and significant to you, you have to follow the process to save and grow your net worth. What choice do you have? So do yourself a favor, whatever you can save today, know that it will grow. And with your next paycheck, and in the next month, and the next year work like hell to make that number grow. Don't let the slow start slow down your life.

Remember This:

- *No one cares about your stuff.*
- *Really, no one cares.*
- *Discipline is a prerequisite for financial stability and independence.*
- *Your level of discipline and ability to ignore the noise of consumerism will determine your success.*

11. Lifestyle inflation is terrifying

If you've read any personal finance-related books or blogs, you've certainly come across the term Lifestyle Inflation or Lifestyle Creep. It's is essentially the upgrading of various things in your life. Trading up from a $10,000 car to a $30,000 one to a $70,000 model. Purchasing Economy Class airfare and then Business Class and then First Class. Eating Ramen Noodles in your dorm room to eating out at the nicest restaurants every night of the week.

Finding Your Purpose and Inspiration

You get the idea. Lifestyle inflation is the result of a few things:

1. Pressure from peers and society to showcase your income level.
2. An internal desire to reward yourself for hard work.
3. A need to give your career progression meaning.
4. The idea that paying for services will save you time or create convenience.

Lifestyle inflation is incredibly dangerous and destructive to your finances and overall wellbeing. But it's also necessary and rewarding. The point of demarcation between positive impacts of inflation and the slippery slope of over-spending is different for everyone, but if you're reading this book and are starting to realize that your spending has gotten away from you, the line was already crossed.

How do you determine where that line is? That's a very personal question, but a good place to start is to ask yourself if the increase in spending is worth more to you now than the freedom in the future. Most people will increase their earnings year-over-year or at least job-over-job. Some lifestyle inflation is a good thing, a great thing in fact! Owning a car or a house, traveling the world, living in a safer or more enjoyable area, providing for your children; all things that most people usually can't do at the start of their very first job, but eventually accumulate the means to do so.

Here's the thing about lifestyle inflation if you let it become normal: it will never be enough. There will always be someone richer, something nicer, more expensive, more luxurious. If you are continually chasing the horizon, you'll never reach it. At some point, you'll need to draw a line in the sand and say, "this is it." There will be a level of expense that should be your target. Let's look at this visually: On the left side of the chart, your costs don't achieve your desired lifestyle because you don't earn enough, but over time, you can reach that point: you can buy a house in the location you want, travel to the places you desire, pursue the activities that bring you the most joy.

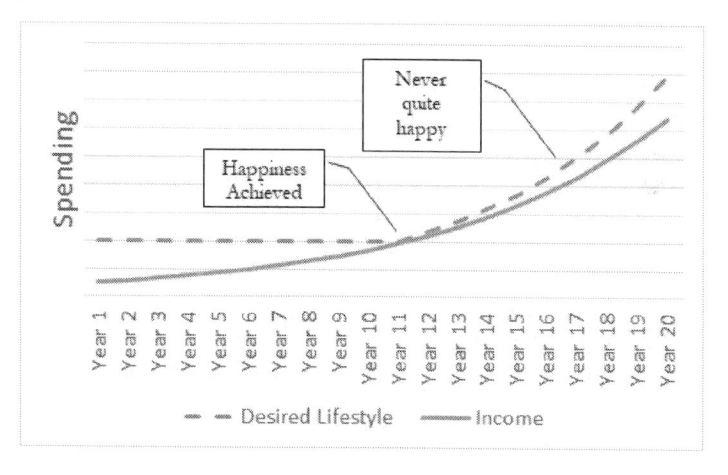

But left unchecked, your spending will increase because it's so easy to spend your money! You'll buy a bigger house, spend more money on your vacations, buy more stuff, etc. And does it make you any happier? Maybe a little here and there, but overall it won't. It may even have an opposite effect on your happiness.

If you don't draw a line and find your level of happiness and spending, your chart will end up looking like this. You'll eventually earn enough to reach what you believed to be your desired lifestyle, but once you get there, you're too focused on what's next. What you think you want and need to be happy is just a little bit out of reach of your expenses, driving you to spend more and more, but never quite achieving it. If you go down this path and fail to adjust, you'll never cross the line again. It will always be out of reach.

When you can identify the desired level of lifestyle spending and hold it steady, not only will you be consistently happy, but your savings rate will skyrocket as that additional income is saved and invested.

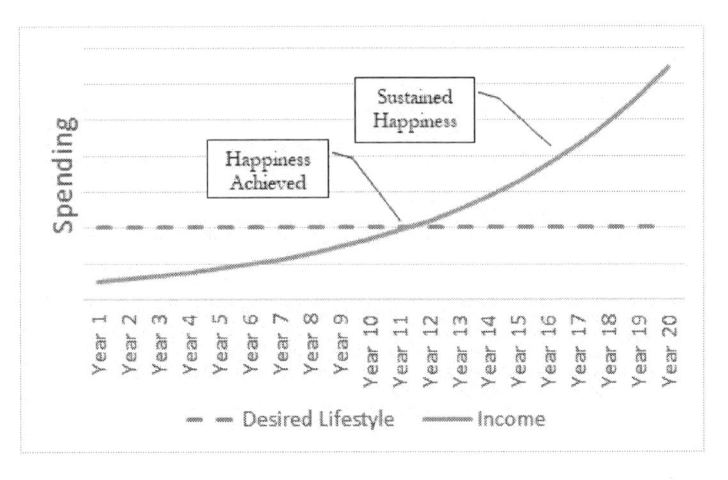

The chart above is academic in its consistency, but it's drawn to illustrate the point. Your real lifestyle line will probably look like this compared to your income. Your desired lifestyle spend increases a little bit each year. And that's totally fine. The point is that your income increases by more than your spending, which means that your rate of savings keeps growing each year.

Your New Relationship With Money

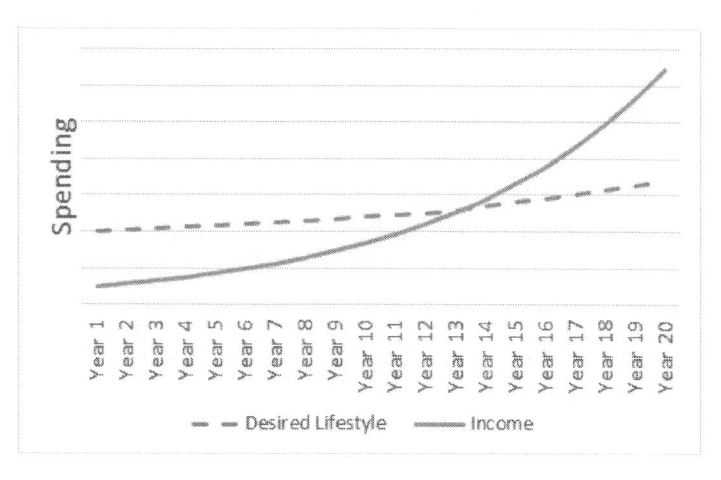

[Chart showing Spending over Year 1 through Year 20, with two lines: "Desired Lifestyle" (dashed) rising gradually, and "Income" (solid) rising slowly at first then steeply, crossing above the Desired Lifestyle line around Year 12.]

Lifestyle inflation isn't a bad thing if monitored and controlled. If it outpaces your earning and savings rates, it can spell disaster. A reasonable rule should be that your savings should increase by the same rate that your income does. If you make $50,000 in year 1, saving $5,000 of it, then in year 2 when you make $55,000, you should save $5,500. This is a 10% savings rate each year as a simple example. That's a good rule, but even saving 10% in the example above isn't enough. At some point, you should find a level of satisfactory lifestyle and stick to it. From that point on, your savings rate as a percentage should keep increasing as your income goes up. It's bad when your savings doesn't increase at all, and it's ugly when your savings decrease because you upgraded your lifestyle too drastically.

Increases in income are very easy excuses to spend your money in the pursuit of lifestyle inflation. I can't tell you how many times I've heard, "I've already spent my bonus" before it's even determined what it is or gets deposited. Earmarking your bonus or using your incremental salary to buy something you didn't have before is what keeps people at a consistently low-level of savings. If last year you saved $10,000 and this year, because of your raise, you <u>could</u> save $11,000, but <u>choose</u> only to save $10,000, that's lifestyle inflation. It's bad news. But once you get to that comfortable lifestyle, you need to lock it down.

I know it's not this simple. There are a million other factors at play, some of which result in unavoidable costs. But the principle is important:

1. Inflate your savings rate faster than you inflate your lifestyle.
2. Find a lifestyle that's sustainable and creates contentment.
3. When it's all said and done, you'll have enough money to do whatever you want in life.

It's ok to want more, to strive for a better life, but don't let that desire get the better of you. Find your happiness and say, "that's enough." There's something quite admirable about knowing yourself and what makes you happy. Conversely, there's something quite tragic about never appreciating what you have.

Remember This:

- *If lifestyle inflation becomes a habit, you'll never have enough.*
- *There will always be someone richer, something nicer, more expensive, more luxurious.*
- *Inflate your savings rate, not your spending rate.*

12. Everything is a trap. A way to separate you from your money.

This chapter will likely be the most cynical of the book, and I don't suggest you go through life thinking everyone is a cheat, and every word is a scam. But there's value in developing and cultivating a critical eye for spending. Not *everything* is a trap, but if you're expecting there to be a trap and actively search for the solution or the best option, there's value in that mentality. Here's the basic logic: If you read or see or hear about something, that message cost someone money. That TV ad, radio spot, flyer in your mailbox or guy on the street corner spinning the sign; those all cost money to deliver to your attention. And if it cost money to tell you something, it is almost certainly because someone hopes to earn more money than they spent by having you act on this new information. You're always being sold something. Not everything is straight-up consumerism though. The government has messages for you, charities ask for your money, your school board needs feedback, etc. But those are the minority. It's best to be a little cynical and view everything as a sneaky way to separate you from your money.

Marketers are experts in convincing you to believe things about other people that aren't true, or about yourself that isn't true. They're experts in convincing you that you need something when you don't, that you'll be happy when you have it, that other people will admire and respect you for buying it. Marketers are experts in convincing you to part with your money.

Finding Your Purpose and Inspiration

Now it would be unfair to say that all marketing is terrible because reading, hearing, or seeing an advertisement might introduce you to something you do value. Something that genuinely was missing from your life. You might find a new source of entertainment, a new hobby, a passion. Developing and cultivating a critical eye doesn't mean that you *dismiss* these messages. You learn to see the truth in them.

But let's be fair to marketers and acknowledge that they earn money, making you part from yours. So be a bit cynical when you come across advertising. Here are a few key categories to be discerning of:

4. **Don't be fooled by the message of saving money.** The sticker price of an item is whatever the seller says it is and they can then advertise any amount of "savings" off that. But in reality, you've saved nothing. You've spent money. You wouldn't have bought that thing that was "50% OFF", so what you've done is wasted money. You've been tricked. The promise of future saving is also almost always a hoax. A portable water filter will save you on future water bottles, but you could also not buy the filter and not buy water bottles. What have you saved?
5. **Attaching aesthetic value to practical items is silly.** There are certain items whose value is aesthetic like art and jewelry, but many things you will buy in your life serve a specific practical purpose. A $5 hammer hits nails just as effectively as the $30 hammer with etched steel, custom leather handle, and chrome head. There is simply no reason to pay $25 for those aesthetic touches.

There is no additional value created from those things; Pretty doesn't equal better.
6. **Scarcity does not indicate value.** Just because an item is a limited time or limited quantity, does not in any way make it more valuable or necessary to you. Even if you do need it, trust me, you'll find it again. And soon. Creating a fear of missing out is a powerful motivator and one that is manipulated to great effect. If a product were so valuable to the public that supply couldn't keep up, the seller of that item would do everything in their power to increase supply. If it's scarce, it likely artificially that way.

There will be times where a product or service you see advertising for will genuinely make your life better. But 99% of the time it won't. Companies have to grow, and that growth comes from reducing costs or increasing revenue. If costs decrease, the consumer is likely getting less. If revenue increases, the consumer is paying more. Healthy skepticism towards marketing and advertising can create significant long-term financial benefit for you.

Remember This:

- *It's best to be a little cynical and view everything as a sneaky way to separate you from your money.*
- *Marketers are experts in convincing you to believe things about other people that aren't true, or about yourself that isn't true.*
- *Discounts, limited time offers, and other advertising terms are artificial and don't create any real benefit to you.*

13. The ever-expanding desire for convenience

Consumers are bombarded with marketing messages extolling the "convenience" of a particular product or service. Jumping at opportunities to make your life more convenient is a costly frame of mind. Just like lifestyle inflation, the need for convenience, if left unchecked, will continue to grow, consuming more of your money and weakening your resolve to push through some inconvenient times. Life isn't easy or convenient, and learning to adapt to and manage those challenges are valuable traits.

Convenience is extremely overrated and the newest tactic of marketers. Let's dig a bit deeper into why this is the case so often. First off, convenience is a different category than what I'm calling "DIY" in a later chapter. There are two primary types of conveniences that people pay for:

1. Outsourcing of Tasks
2. Modification or Simplification of Activities

Regarding the first item, these are the things that don't require a high level of knowledge, expertise, or time. Let's define and differentiate these by calling convenience items "tasks" and knowledge items "skills." Mowing a lawn is a task, but having someone fix the engine on your lawnmower is a skill. Installing drywall in your home is a skill, but rolling paint onto the wall it is a task. Buying groceries is a task, as is walking the dog, cleaning the house, etc.

Convenience costs money. Not only are you usually paying for someone else's labor, but you're paying a premium on top of that. Using the lawn mowing example, you're paying for the worker to mow it and the overhead of the company that manages that labor for you. Having your groceries delivered is the same thing: you pay for the worker to go pick out your food and bring it to your home, and you're also paying for the company who set up the whole operation and to advertise to you.

Sooner or later, you might find yourself with a lawnmower, grocery deliverer, house cleaner, laundry service, and how much time have you saved? Does that free time translate into more money? Or can you now pursue your passions more thoroughly? My guess is that despite all these conveniences, your time is still consumed and you feel busy managing all these external services. Like the goldfish who grows to the size of his bowl, so too will your everyday commitments consume your time. The endless search for more conveniences and the managing of all those services will continue to tax your time and energy.

In isolation, a single service might not seem like that big of a deal. $40 to mow the lawn each week? Not too expensive. But that's $40 for the grass, $30 for the landscaping, $100 for the house cleaning, and in the end, you're spending hundreds a week, which is thousands a year. Maybe there is a task or two that you find too painful to do yourself; that's ok! Pick the convenience of services that do add value to your life; just don't make a habit of it. If the thought of cleaning leaves from your gutter fills you with dread, hire someone. But if every task fills you with dread, try to address your underlying aversion to labor. It will only get worse if you don't.

The 2nd area of convenience spending is the modification or simplification of an activity that is for any number of reasons disagreeable; taking a cab instead of the train, popping in a single-serve coffee cup instead of filtering the grounds, using a vegetable dicer instead of cutting it yourself. These types of conveniences aren't *always* a bad thing, but making them the rule as opposed to the exception is what you should avoid. Travel is a perfect example of how convenience can become a sizeable expense. You can take the train to the airport, check-in, and board with the masses, sit in the Economy and get the airport shuttle to the hotel once you get there. Or you can get a private car, go through security via the priority lanes because you bought a First Class ticket, board first, deplane first, get your bag first and get another private car to your hotel. It sounds nice, but how much nicer does it make your travel day? Maybe a little bit nicer, but is it worth the extra $5,000? If you travel alone and only once a year, perhaps it is. But if you travel with a family and do it frequently, this sort of moderate improvement to your trip will start to have significant repercussions on your finances.

But it's one of my spending priorities, you say! That's why you are traveling and why you should feel good about the efficiency of your spending. Don't use your spending priorities as an excuse to splurge unnecessarily. We're not talking about buying tickets to the Louvre or a rafting trip down the Colorado River; we're talking about the unnecessary convenience purchases along the way.

Saving money isn't the only issue, though. It's about developing a tolerance for challenging situations, to find enjoyment in completing difficult or stressful tasks. There are satisfaction and fulfillment in staring down a challenge and knowing you can overcome it yourself. Maybe it's a 24-hour travel day with toddlers in tow, perhaps it's the 5-hour cleaning marathon of the grout in your bathroom, or it could be the daunting task of planning your financial future. Saving money aside, completing inconvenient tasks, and surviving uncomfortable situations will not only make you more capable, but it will increase your enjoyment for later convenience purchases.

Activity or event-based conveniences are easier to discern than the tiny conveniences built into the things we use daily. Having a coffee machine is great, but do you need the one that simplifies the brewing process into a single step? Does the milk-warmer help you out a lot? What about the wireless-enabled controls that start brewing when your alarm goes off in the morning? These things come at a cost and will lead to more complexity in your life. Simple machines have fewer points of failure, whereas complex mechanical, electrical, and computing devices can fail at any number of points. The time needed to set up, to maintain and to eventually fix these issues will probably take more time away from you over the machine's life than a simple one would, despite the promise of convenience. So pour some grounds and brew the simple pot of coffee. Everything will be fine.

If you have kids, consider for a moment the double standard: we make our kids endure every aspect of education, regardless of if they enjoy it. We make them study, produce homework, memorize words and equations, and that's not even including sports. They train and condition and practice, sweating, suffering injuries, crying, throwing up and losing games. And at home, they do chores, clean up their rooms, take out the trash, and finish their dinner plates. These are all horribly inconvenient for kids.

Childhood is structured around teaching kids the skills needed to survive life and be productive. Children are put into inconvenient situations because it forces them to learn and adapt and most importantly, develop a tolerance for more learning and more adaptation. The crazy thing about adulthood is that the need to learn and the necessity of adaptation don't end when your paychecks start. They get more frequent and the implications become much more severe. Just because you can afford to outsource tasks or buy your way into comfort, doesn't mean you should. In the same way that we teach our kids to be self-reliant and resilient, so too should adults continue that philosophy.

Remember This:

- *Convenience costs money.*
- *Despite all these conveniences, your time is still consumed and you feel busy managing all these external services.*
- *Completing inconvenient tasks and surviving uncomfortable situations will make you more capable.*

14. Understand how you spend money

Financial independence requires money, and you have to earn that. But how much do you need? Only when you understand your expenses can you answer that question. A goal of retirement and financial independence without a firm grasp on your spending is entirely futile. It's a shot in the dark.

Most of the financial advice online is total crap. People give you targets and tricks and tips, but not only is it sometimes misleading, but it can also be wrong! Saving money is desperately simple: don't spend it. It may take sacrifices to cut out of your life the things you have purchased for so long. It's simple, though. How much money you need to be financially independent is unique to everyone. It's a balance of the lifestyle you want and the sacrifices you're willing to make now and in perpetuity.

Finding Your Purpose and Inspiration

The second most crucial step toward financial independence, a very close second after adopting a net worth view, is to track your spending. From this, you can determine not only how much you need, but how fast you'll get it. I like to use an overly simple formula to ground myself: savings rate divided by spending rate. We'll exclude taxes for simplicity, but the principle is the same regardless of the nuances.

It calculates how much of a year's worth of expenses you save in one year. If you save 50% of your income, one year of working and savings equals one year of financial independence. This is because the 50% you saved, means you spent 50%. So you now have enough remaining from that one year of working to cover one year of expenses. Of course, this doesn't account for inflation or investments, etc., but I like the idea. It also assumes that your level of spending is what you need to live your desired lifestyle.

Let's first look at this very unrealistically to convey the point: you earn $1 million a year. And you spend $100,000. After one year, you have a net of $900,000 (forget taxes for a minute). With that $900,000, you can continue your current lifestyle for nine years. That's an unrealistic scenario, so let's consider a more likely circumstance.

If you're saving 10% of your income, that means you need to work nine years to save up enough to equal one year of spending (which is 90% of your income). That's scary. But anything over the 50% mark and you're now buying more time than you're putting in. If you were to save 90% of your income, the opposite of the above example, you then create nine years of financial independence after one year

Your New Relationship With Money

of working. Using real dollars: if you earn $100,000 dollars, saving $60,000 and spending $40,000, that $60,000 of savings is 1.5 years' worth of expenses ($60,000/$40,000). Of course, this assumes that you can maintain the lifestyle which created the savings rate. So you can't save like crazy for a year and then start spending again. Your spending must be sustainable.

Take a look at the table below and find the percentage savings rate you are currently at:

Savings Rate	Years of Financial Independence	Years Needed to Save 1 Year of Expenses
5%	0.05	19.00
10%	0.11	9.00
15%	0.18	5.67
20%	0.25	4.00
25%	0.33	3.00
30%	0.43	2.33
35%	0.54	1.86
40%	0.67	1.50
45%	0.82	1.22
50%	1.00	1.00
55%	1.22	0.82
60%	1.50	0.67
65%	1.86	0.54
70%	2.33	0.43
75%	3.00	0.33
80%	4.00	0.25
85%	5.67	0.18
90%	9.00	0.11
95%	19.00	0.05

Finding Your Purpose and Inspiration

I like this view because it's good motivation: either negative or positive. If you keep saving and continue to grow your income, you'll be earning more and more time. If you can get to a 50% savings rate, that would mean each year of work equals one year of not working. And that's just dollar-for-dollar! It will, of course, grow over time, perhaps yielding 2 or 3 years of expenses depending on how early in your life you invest this. That's a pretty good motivator, in my opinion.

If you're only saving 6% of your income into a 401k and spending every remaining penny you make, you'll need to think hard about your retirement strategy. If you're young, that 6% *may* grow to be enough after 40 years of working. It may not. If you can save more, you may not even need 40 years to let it grow.

You earn money, and you spend money. The former is hard to control, which makes the latter the key to this whole equation. It's important to reframe your concept of spending. If looking at that chart makes you anxious, that's the point. And conversely, if looking at that chart gives you pride and satisfaction, that's also the point. There is no right percent to save and no right amount to spend. But when you understand your spending through the lens of financial independence, it's a powerful motivator.

Remember This:

- *If you save 10% of your income and spend 90%, you need nine years to save the amount you spend in one year.*
- *If you save 90% of your income and spend 10%, you will save nine years' worth of spend in one year.*
- *There is no magic savings rate and anyone telling you what it should be is probably wrong.*

15. Discover your inner DIY

In chapter 13, we discussed convenience and the difference between a task and a skill, so now let's focus on the benefits of learning the latter. Completing easy tasks can save you money and also build up a tolerance for a challenge in your life, but learning a new skill and becoming a Do-It-Yourself-er (DIYer) can provide even more satisfaction and fulfillment. If mowing your lawn is a task, then repairing your lawnmower is DIY. Taking apart a lawnmower and repairing it takes knowledge and skill. If you choose to acquire neither of them, you'll pay someone not just for their time, but also their experience and their expertise to fix it. Convenience tasks are relatively inexpensive, but paying for skills can be costly.

To be clear, though, you have to draw a clear line for what you should learn and what you must avoid. Climbing up to the street's electrical transformer to get your power

Finding Your Purpose and Inspiration

back on is super dangerous, don't DIY that. And repairing your roof, another no-no. Building a lead-acid battery for your car, please don't. Don't risk your life or financial ruin to be a DIYer.

Here's a little decision tree to help you out:

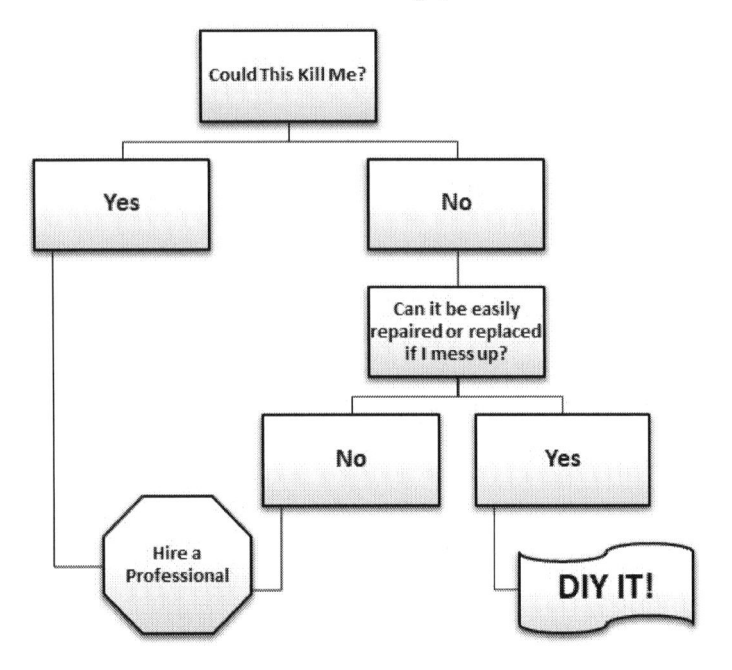

```
                    ┌──────────────────┐
                    │ Could This Kill Me? │
                    └──────────────────┘
                     /              \
                    /                \
            ┌─────────┐         ┌─────────┐
            │   Yes   │         │   No    │
            └─────────┘         └─────────┘
                                      │
                            ┌──────────────────┐
                            │  Can it be easily │
                            │ repaired or replaced │
                            │   if I mess up?  │
                            └──────────────────┘
                              /          \
                        ┌─────────┐   ┌─────────┐
                        │   No    │   │   Yes   │
                        └─────────┘   └─────────┘
                             │              │
                    ┌──────────────┐    ┌─────────┐
                    │    Hire a    │    │ DIY IT! │
                    │ Professional │    └─────────┘
                    └──────────────┘
```

Almost everything will fall into the DIY category. Of course there is a risk that you'll irreparably harm whatever you are DIYing, and you'll need to hire a professional then or buy a new item, but think about the real risk: If you DIY 10 items and 1 gets messed up, you are still better off than outsourcing or replacing all 10 and not even trying to DIY.

In most cases, you can attempt to DIY without risking anything, and the worst that will happen is that you learn a little about what you're facing and are better equipped for the future. Let's take a few examples:

The kitchen faucet is leaking:

- Step 1: Visit YouTube.com and type in "The kitchen faucet is leaking."
- Step 2: Click on the first of over 100,000 videos
- Step 3: Explore the faucet, check for the common issues identified in the video and find the problem
- Step 4: Tighten the pipes, replace the $0.50 o-ring, etc.

You just saved $200 to get someone out to fix it! Now if it turns out that your pipes are old and have corroded and need to be replaced in the whole kitchen, then maybe call someone.

My printer doesn't print:

- Step 1: Visit YouTube.com and type in "My (Insert model number) printer doesn't print."
- Step 2: Click on the first of over 100,000 videos
- Step 3: Follow the instructions
- Step 4: download the right drivers, uninstall/reinstall, replace the $2 USB cable, etc.

You just saved $100 replacing your printer! I think you can see where this is going.

If plumbing or computers scare you, don't be intimidated. YouTube is the best thing that's ever happened to DIYers. You will learn everything. And perhaps you research how to build your backyard playground and decide that you'd rather not risk having to tear it down due to poor craftsmanship, that's ok. Give yourself a chance to learn it though. Build a chair first and then a ladder and work your way up. Even if you don't DIY a particular thing, you are now more knowledgeable about what it takes to do it. You can manage whomever you hire more effectively; you can more accurately identify the right replacement, etc. If the plumber tells you that you need a new faucet, but you know it's just an o-ring, you can challenge the recommendation and not get screwed. You will be better off in almost every situation if you at least try to DIY.

And if you fix the sink, reinstall the printer, hang the drywall and build that playground, you will have saved a ton of money and feel tremendous satisfaction. You'll have those skills for the rest of your life. Not only can you deploy them when needed to save money, but those skills make you a smarter consumer. If you've spent years doing your plumbing and repairing drywall, when you get a quote from a contractor to do an addition to your house, you'll have exponentially more knowledge by which to discern the quality of that quote.

Practical value aside, learning new skills, developing unique expertise, and becoming more self-sufficient is extremely rewarding. You spend years learning skills and building knowledge at work, and much of it is invaluable. But most of it is entirely useless the second you leave that job. The skills you learn for your own life can provide value forever. Consider putting forth just a fraction of the effort you display at work to learn new skills outside of it. You should always attempt to learn something new before deciding to outsource the work.

Your New Relationship With Money

Manual labor aside, the one thing you should absolutely learn to DIY and always do yourself is personal finance. Do-It-Yourself finance is the essence of this book! Not only will you save money, but you'll be able to plan your future, adapt to change, capitalize on opportunities, hedge against risk, and you won't go through life confused about this significant category of your life: money. Some of the topics in this book you may find too complicated or risky to do yourself, and that's perfectly fine. But learn about them first. Try to do them yourself first. You'll be better because of it.

This new relationship with money also requires new skills and the right tools. Let's begin.

Remember This:

- *If a DIY project can kill you, don't even attempt it.*
- *If it can't kill you and you can't burn your house down from it, attempt it.*
- *Even if you don't complete the DIY project, you'll be more knowledgeable and better informed than you were before you started.*

Finding Your Purpose and Inspiration

Part 3
Understanding the Tools You'll Need

16. Compounding growth rates

I was having lunch with a friend of mine, and I expressed my disappointment in the sandwich I was eating, which had cost me $10. It was a rip-off, I proclaimed. After I swore to never eat at that place again, he said, "You know that sandwich just cost you $10,000 in retirement savings..."

What he was alluding to was the power of compounding growth. Read almost anything on personal finance, and you'll undoubtedly be presented with a recommendation on how to best grow your money over time via compounding. The concept is simple: A dollar invested today at a 10% growth rate can become $1.10 next year and $1.21 and so on. In 30 years, that dollar is worth multiples of what it was when you invested it because you are continually earning 10% of an ever-growing number. 10% of a dollar is $0.10. But 10% of $1.10 the next year is $0.11. Growth upon growth is compounding. Here is a visual:

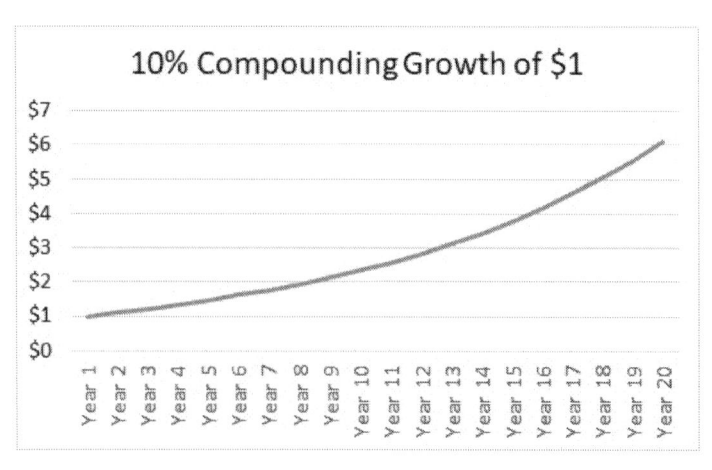

In 20 years that $1 is worth over $6. Now imagine if instead of $1 it was $1,000 or $100,000. The increases are small at first, but fast-forward many years and that 10% is a material amount of money. The percentage stays the same, but the dollar amount grows each period.

You've probably seen articles that present attractive what-if scenarios like "if you had bought Apple when…" or "if invested during the bottom of the recession you'd have…" Although these scenarios are extreme, this is how investments work. Money grows over time, and the longer it stays invested, the more it grows. What starts small can grow large if it stays invested and the earnings compound upon one another.

Back to the sandwich: It wasn't very good, which made it worse, but the math is what irked me. At 8% annual returns, that $10 would be worth about $100 in 30 years. Is the sandwich worth $100? Of course not! You'll make yourself crazy thinking this way about every dollar, but the compounding effect of investing means there is more money in the future than there is today.

But you should think about the future value of money for larger purchases, especially the substantial purchases that come around occasionally. While a $10 lunch is one of those things that you have to accept as the cost of living, many purchases should be scrutinized a little more. Cars are the easiest example. An extra $20,000 for a luxury car could be $200,000 in 30 years. Even something like a new washing machine can be a big deal. Spending $2,000 instead of $500? That's a $20,000 washing machine.

Understanding the Tools You'll Need

When it comes to saving for retirement, small contributions can grow over a long period. But if you are close to retirement age, you'll need to save exponentially more because it won't have the time to grow. Let's look at two examples with numbers and then a visual. If you're 30 years old and want to have an investment grow to $1 million by age 60, you'll need to invest $57,000 assuming a constant 10% growth. If you're 40, you'll need to invest $148,000. If you're 50 and want a single investment to hit $1 million by age 60, you'll need $386,000.

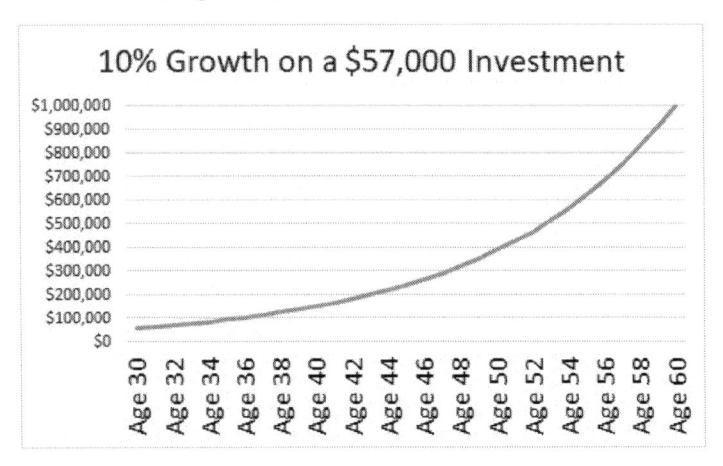

10% Growth on a $57,000 Investment

[Chart showing exponential growth from $0 at Age 30 to $1,000,000 at Age 60]

This example doesn't factor in contributing money to an investment each year, which is what you'll be doing over time. As you can see though, in the same way that the $1 grows from the earlier example, the longer the money stays invested, the higher the return each year as a dollar amount.

If you're disciplined enough to be able to save a considerable amount for retirement early in your life and continue to do so year after year, you'll be considerably wealthy down the road. Every day you postpone this saving in investing will be reflected in real and very large dollar amounts later in your life. It's important not to get discouraged early on in this journey. This relationship with money might have a slow start, but you'll get there.

Remember This:

- *Start investing early!*
- *Compounding growth is when you continue to invest your returns which then also begin generating returns of their own. This growth accelerates over time.*
- *Generally speaking from the long-term performance of the stock market, the longer you maintain your investments, the greater your return will be.*
- *$1 saved and invested now will grow to be a material amount of money in the future.*
- *Consider the future value of money before spending it.*

17. Learning Excel and basic math

As we discussed in chapter 15 about becoming a DIYer, it's imperative that you develop a working knowledge of basic financial concepts and the ability to calculate, record and analyze numbers in Microsoft Excel or similar spreadsheet software. If your palms get sweaty and your heart skips a beat thinking about Excel, I have bad news and good news: the bad news is that if you want to manage numbers, you need Excel. The good news is that you can learn this program. And when in doubt, visit YouTube or MrExcel.com.

When it comes to personal finance and Excel, there are two types of calculations that you'll be using the most: Summing expenses and calculating future values of assets. The next two chapters will focus on these use-cases, but to effectively manage them, you'll need the technical skills. Let's take a look at the expense part because it's the easiest. I'm going to keep this brief with the intention that you can develop a baseline understanding of the program and then teach yourself through practice and additional research on how to be proficient.

	A	B	C	D	E
1					
2					
3					
4					
5					
6					

The basic mechanics of excel work like algebra. "=" starts an equation, followed by the numbers and the actions. =10*10 is ten multiplied by 10. =10/10 is 10 divided by 10. "+" and "-" are what you'd expect. You can then reference other cells in the file to do your calculations. The left-hand column of the table has numbers, and the top row has letters. A1 is the top-left cell. A2 is one below. =10*A1 where A1 has 10 in it, calculates out the multiplication of 10 times 10.

Summing expenses allows you to understand totals: totals by month, totals by year, by category, etc. In Excel, list out the items you want to see the combined value for. To calculate something, the number must be in its own cell. The formula is then: =SUM(Cell 1, Cell 2, Cell 3, Etc.).

Understanding the Tools You'll Need

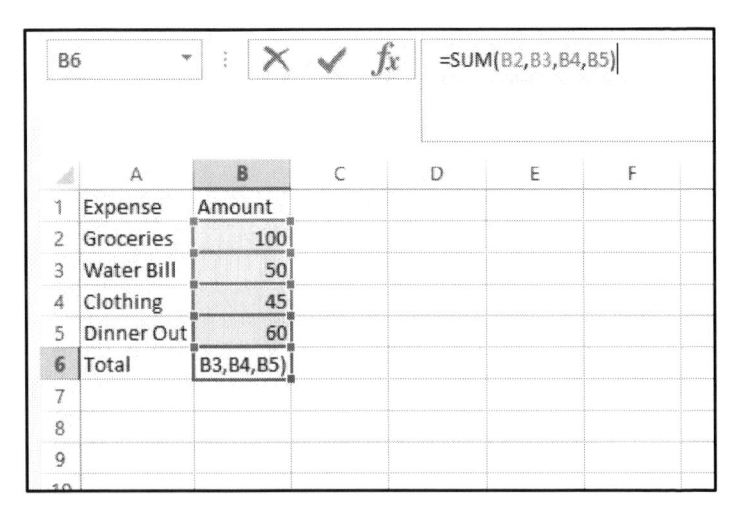

[Screenshot of Excel spreadsheet with formula bar showing =SUM(B2,B3,B4,B5) and cell B6 selected containing B3,B4,B5)]

	A	B
1	Expense	Amount
2	Groceries	100
3	Water Bill	50
4	Clothing	45
5	Dinner Out	60
6	Total	B3,B4,B5)

You can also highlight a section of adjacent cells with the SUM function.

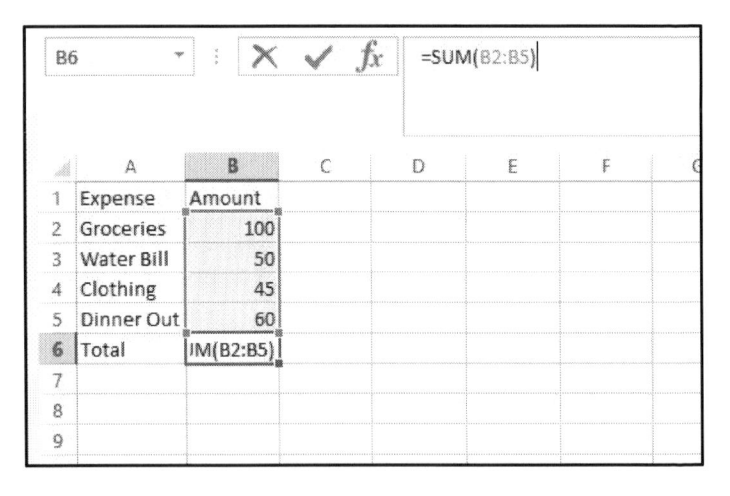

[Screenshot of Excel spreadsheet with formula bar showing =SUM(B2:B5) and cell B6 selected]

	A	B
1	Expense	Amount
2	Groceries	100
3	Water Bill	50
4	Clothing	45
5	Dinner Out	60
6	Total	JM(B2:B5)

With this formula, you can track your assets and your expenses. By creating different lists, it's easy to see numbers in the aggregate, which is impactful. In the example above, one receipt for a $60 dinner might not bother you, but seeing 100 dinners out over 12 months will likely give you pause.

Excel isn't so hard, right?

The other principal type of calculation is for future values, which can be an asset's value after years of a specified interest rate, or the cost of credit card debt, or an anticipated growth rate of your investment accounts.

Let's say you want to do some quick math to see how much your retirement portfolio will be worth in 30 years. You'll need the expected annual return in the market, let's call it 7%, the number of years, 30, how much you contribute annually, $10,000, and the current value of your investments, $100,000.

- **Formula:** =FV(rate,nper,pmt,[pv],[type])
- **Translation:** =Future Value(growth rate, time periods, annual contribution, present value, if growth is applied at the beginning or the end of the period)
- **The Numbers:** =FV(0.07,30,10000,100000,0)
- **The Answer:** $1,705,833, which is how much money you'd have after 30 years.

To be clear, this is not a realistic scenario where you have a constant growth rate. Some years will be up, some down. But generally speaking, this formula is a great way to get a directional answer to a future value scenario.

Another incredibly useful formula is the calculation of a loan payment. It's very similar to the FV formula if you want to calculate the payment on a loan, such as a mortgage. A note on interest rates: An interest rate of 4%

Understanding the Tools You'll Need

on loan is typically divided by 12 months to get a monthly rate. 4% would be 0.33% monthly. There is a difference between 4% incurred for one year vs. 0.33% incurred monthly. And as you can imagine, when someone gives you a 4% loan, it works out to be a higher number. It's never in your favor.

Here is a monthly payment calculation for a 30-year (360 months), $300,000 mortgage with a 4% interest rate:

- **Formula:** =PMT(rate,nper,pv,[fv],[type])
- **Translation:** =Payment(growth rate, periods, starting loan amount, remaining loan at the end of the team, if growth is applied at the beginning or the end of the period)
- **The Numbers:** =PMT(0.04/12,360,300000,0,1)
- **The Answer:** $1,427, which is how much you'd owe monthly to pay off this loan in 30 years.

Excel is an extremely powerful and resourceful tool, but you don't need to be an expert to get a lot of value from it. It's important that if you don't feel confident with math and Excel that you learn. It's not that you'll need to do complicated math in your head or risk a financial catastrophe; you need to familiarize yourself with the components of everyday situations you're facing. You won't need to do advanced real-time algebra at the car dealership, but you'll need to know what the salesperson is talking about to spot the catch.

Many websites and apps will do these things for you, but I encourage you to learn it yourself first. You'll need it for the rest of this book's subjects.

Remember This:

- *Basic Excel is something you can definitely learn.*
- *You won't need to be an expert, but understanding how calculations work will help you in all of life's financial situations.*
- *Building your own Excel tools will help you learn and develop an intimate understanding of your money.*

18. The most important tool there is

Now that you have a basic knowledge of Excel, it's time to build your net worth chart. If you're thinking that manually creating a chart is more difficult than an automatic option online such as mint.com, you're right. But there is a purpose to this, and it's impactful. If you create a net worth chart online simply by connecting your various accounts, you lose the connection, both visually and figuratively to the underlying detail of each account. You can't just log in periodically, see that you have a little more money and then call it a day. There is little value in solely knowing how much you have. The value comes from understanding what you have, how each piece moves relative to your other assets, how it changes over time, and where you are weak and strong. The bottom line is that you must do this yourself, do it regularly and for a long time—forever really.

Understanding the Tools You'll Need

Let me create a new paragraph here to reiterate the importance of this point: you must do this manually, consistently, and forever. It is the most critical tool you will have in developing a new relationship with money.

It's not too hard though, so let's jump in with an example. Don't worry though; we will build one of these step-by-step together later in the book.

Retirement Accounts					$35K
401k	$20K	Pension	$9K	Roth IRA	$4K
Large Cap ETF	$5K	Cash Balance	$5K	Large Cap ETF	$1K
Small Cap ETF	$5K			Small Cap ETF	$1K
Dividend ETF	$5K	Health Savings Account	$2K	Dividend ETF	$1K
S&P 500 ETF	$5K	Cash Balance	$2K	S&P 500 ETF	$1K

Non-Retirement Assets					$39K
Brokerage Account	$12K	Checking Account	$10K	529 Plan	$8K
Large Cap ETF	$3K	Cash Balance	$10K	Large Cap ETF	$8K
Small Cap ETF	$3K				
Dividend ETF	$3K	Deferred Income Plan	$3K	Company Stock Plan	$6K
S&P 500 ETF	$3K	Cash Balance	$3K	Shares	$6K

Real Estate				$100K
Home	$300K	Mortgage	($200K)	
Market Value	$300K	Remaining Balance	($200K)	

Short-Term Liabilities					($73K)
Credit Cards	($2K)	Car Loans	($21K)	Student Loans	($50K)
Visa	($1K)	Car 1	($10K)	Remaining Balance	($50K)
Mastercard	($1K)	Car 2	($11K)		

Other Assets				$27K
Cars	$27K	Other	$4K	
Car 1	$12K	Jewelry	$2K	
Car 2	$15K	Art	$2K	
		Other	$1K	

TOTAL NET WORTH	$129K
Retirement	$35K
Cash Investments	$20K
Available Cash	$10K

The numbers are placeholders only, so don't look at them comparatively to your situation. If you're married, you should have one chart for the household so you might have two IRA's, two cars, etc. If your spouse has a separate checking account that you're not allowed to see, work through those marital trust issues and then capture it on the single net worth cart. You need to capture everything.

You may ask why you need a chart for this. Maybe you log into your checking account or 401k every month, and it's in great shape. People pose that to me that all the time and the answer is that one account is not an indicator of your overall financial health. It doesn't allow you to look at your entire "portfolio" and make strategic decisions. Mortgage payments showcase this benefit: when you track your liabilities, like a mortgage or car payment, a reduction in that liability is a gain in your net worth. If you have a $2,000 mortgage payment and $1,000 of that is principal, then despite "spending" $2,000 in cash, your net worth only decreases by $1,000. The $1,000 principal payment moves from your checking account cell in the spreadsheet to your mortgage balance. The other $1,000 for interest and taxes is an expense, and you don't get that back, but the principal payment is now your equity in the house. You have $1,000 more ownership of the house.

Another mortgage example would be a one-time payment. Let's say that you have $10,000 extra in a checking account and want to pay down your mortgage: you give that money to the lender, so the cash is gone, and it's removed from your checking out both physically and in the chart. But now your mortgage liability decreases by $10,000, meaning that you own more of the house than you did before. The net impact of this on the net worth chart is zero. The benefit to you is that you're now paying less interest over time to the bank, which is great. You're also closer to being mortgage-free and having lower monthly cash needs. If you weren't actively tracking this in your net worth chart, you would probably feel like the money evaporated from your life.

If you remember the examples from Chapter 8 on net worth for the $100 of income, you could either enter $75 in the checking account cell or $106 in the 401k cell. If you have a net worth mindset, you'll choose the higher number decision every time and watch that total net worth number grow. Being out of sight and therefore out of mind is a hurdle for many people and you can address this psychological issue with the net worth chart. For many, putting money into a 401k or a 529 college savings account means kissing it goodbye. If you're 25, putting money into a 401k means not touching it for 35 years. But not seeing it and not managing it are two very different behaviors. When you are forced to open your 401k account and make a record of all your investments each month, it not only allows you to manage that money more effectively, but it brings you closer to it figuratively. You see it every month and watch it grow. After a few months of this, you won't feel like you've said goodbye to your money. On the contrary, you'll feel a close relationship with that money.

In addition to the immediate benefits I previously mentioned, the net worth view of your life lets you take advantage of all kinds of situations, big and small. For example, if a credit card offers a 5% cashback bonus on electric bills paid for a limited time, you can prepay a year's worth of charges and earn yourself a 5% bonus. On the net worth chart, you tally this expense as positive balance since you know that A) you'll deplete it in a year of average bills from the electric company or B) you switch utility companies, and you get a check back for the balance. That positive balance on your electric bill account is just another little bank account. You see an instant 5% bonus, not the cash expenses. If you can give up cash now and effectively earn it back over time, you can make money doing that. It's the same as a bank giving you cash, and then you paying it back with interest over time. But because the net worth chart records both assets and liabilities, you can recognize opportunities to earn a small return on your purchases. It might be $5 or $10 or maybe $10,000; you need to look for them.

The net worth chart should be tracked monthly. And religiously! Pick a day every month, check the balance of every account you own and enter it in a spreadsheet. It's essential to do it every month, and on the same day because only then can you track your results and make decisions. Tracking every day will make you go crazy with market swings and tracking every year doesn't allow you to make changes as quickly and responsively as you will need to. And you should track on the same day each month to normalize expenses and income.

For example, if one month you record the values of accounts after 30 days, you'll have one mortgage payment, two paychecks, etc. But if the next month, you do 45 days, you'll have one mortgage payment and three paychecks. Depending on your situation, this could create a false sense of net worth growth pacing. More importantly, though, you should develop the discipline to do this exercise every month.

Speaking of discipline, don't take short cuts. Don't put your checking account balance at $1,000 when it's $1,004 because you don't want to log into your account. It probably won't make a difference in your growth number, but over time, your shortcuts will get larger and larger, and the resulting chart won't represent reality. You'll miss a fraudulent charge on your credit card statement, a rogue fee in your checking account, a massive drop in your checking account and other events. You might cut corners on a few dollars, but over time, that will increase to hundreds of dollars and then thousands. At that point, the value is lost.

Another pitfall to avoid is unrealistic assessments of assets. Don't value your house $50,000 over the comparable sales because you did a significant renovation. Don't appraise your jewelry at 5X their true resale value because of sentimental reasons. Do the research and determine true market value. No one will see this chart except you, so don't lie to yourself.

I challenge you to track your net worth. You might find out that you have much more money than you think. You might also scare yourself into some better savings habits. Track this for a few months and see what kind of growth you see. If you see a decline, read the next chapter on spending and then track your net worth again. When it comes to money, it doesn't matter how much you earn, or what you own, or appear to own. It's not your title or benefits. Your net worth is what matters, and all your energy should be focused on this objective.

Money sitting in your checking account provides the least growth opportunity, so look at your chart and find the best location for that money to grow. You have one goal: Grow every month. First, you may only grow by 0.1% a month, but that will change. Track this and then set an annual goal, a strategy I'll discuss in chapter 30.

Remember This:

- *Creating and then regularly updating a net worth chart creates a feeling of ownership vs. automation solutions.*
- *A net worth chart, reviewed regularly, enables you to make strategic decisions through intentional organization.*
- *Stick with it for three months and you'll see a change in your thinking.*
- *It is the most important tool you have.*

19. Keep track of your spending

Tracking your net worth is the most important activity you can do to change your mind set about money and to plot the best trajectory toward financial success. A close second is tracking your spending. The net worth chart helps facilitate maximum effectiveness and growth of your assets, but understanding your spending is how you turn those assets into *time* and financial independence. How many months of "emergency savings" do you have? How many years can your 401k support you in retirement? If you don't know the answer, you probably lack a clear view of your spending. If you have $100,000 in cash, that could

Understanding the Tools You'll Need

be two years of living expenses at $50,000 a year. Or maybe one year. Or 3 months? You won't know until you track your spending. Even if you have a number in your head right now, I promise you it's off by a considerable amount. The whole consumer economy is built around you not scrutinizing your expenses.

- We'll go through the mechanics of how to set up an expense tracking later in this book, so for now, let's focus on the outcome of this activity:
- You'll clearly see where you're wasting money and where you should focus your attention to save.
- You'll clearly see what your lifestyle costs and what you need long term to live.

The first bullet makes a lot of sense, obviously, but it's the second bullet that will yield a profound effect. Together, they are the key to financial independence, and I think you should give it a try. Now the unfortunate truth is that if you're not willing to track every expense, you're not going to be willing to analyze the way you spend and save money. And if you don't analyze the way you spend and save money, you'll never understand what it is you need to change. Even if you accidentally stumble upon those things, chances are you won't be willing to change it. Keeping a spreadsheet is much, much easier than committing to a significant lifestyle deflation based on what you learn. So if you won't keep a spreadsheet, and won't make tough choices with your spending, you'll stay beholden to a paycheck until the day you die. Or until you have an epiphany. So I encourage you to give this a try.

Once you commit to tracking your expenses and categorizing them, things start to make a lot of sense. Of course, there are the big things like mortgages and insurance, school, groceries, utilities; those are ones you are likely aware of, but even then, see one enormous annual number for "utilities" and trust me, you'll want to find a way to cut back. And what about the little stuff? All those coffees and granola bars, the dry cleaning, the Girl Scout Cookies, the parking fees, the lawn service, batteries for the toys, HDMI cables for the TVs; those are the things you never track. And they add up.

When I first compiled a detailed tracker of my family's annual costs of living, it was staggering. And I'm the guy writing a book about saving money. Now maybe what I find staggering and you find staggering is different, but the point is, I was shocked. However, everything changed for me. I became much more conscious and sensitive about spending, especially those expenses which are recurring. If you track your electric bill all summer and painfully type those numbers into a spreadsheet, you'll start using the air conditioner less.

The first order of business is to start cutting down unnecessarily high expenses that otherwise went unnoticed. Take your car and homeowner's insurance and shop around. Switch grocery stores. Eat out at restaurants less. Scrutinize your medical bills. Reduce your impulse shopping. Look for alternate sources of entertainment that don't cost an arm and a leg. Do these things, and you'll save money.

We talked about lifestyle inflation earlier in the book, and one major factor is that when new expenses begin in your life, you don't cut out the old ones. For example, if you have kids, you'll be faced with daycare expenses that didn't

Understanding the Tools You'll Need

exist in your life before. But now that you're a parent and you're buying diapers, and baby food are you also still going to the gym with your $50 a month membership? Are you utilizing your $150 a month cable TV package when you only watch football on the weekends? And when was the last time you enjoyed your wine of the month? Well, maybe with kids you enjoy the wine more. Hopefully, you get the idea: your expenses will change over time, and so you should always be evaluating what's important. If you always add and never subtract, you'll be 70 and still receive your print copy of Sports Illustrated.

So now that you're tracking expenses, understanding your needs and making decisions to improve your spending habits, what's next? This brings me to the truly impactful result of this activity: how much money you need. By knowing how much you need to live a happy life, you can plan your future. If I were to ask you how much money it would take to never need another paycheck and live your ideal lifestyle, what would your answer be? Likely, it would be something arbitrary. And if it's arbitrary, you're bound to work way too long or not nearly long enough.

If spending $100,000 a year meant that you had to work until 73 to save enough money, what does spending $50,000 a year mean? If you can know your spending and then improve your saving, you get the double benefit of knowing what you need to do to achieve financial independence and get there quicker.

For the example above, let's use a common retirement rule called The 4% Rule, which says that you can withdraw 4% of your investment portfolio each year and you will never run out of money. The rule assumes that your money has grown and replenishes most or all of what you withdrew. Using numbers, this means you need $2.5 million to retire at whatever age if you are withdrawing $100,000 a year. At $50,000, you need $1.25 million. $50,000 divided by 4% equals $1.25 million. How many years of earning and saving is that? A few no doubt. And what if you didn't have a mortgage and didn't have car payments, what then? Could you live off $30,000? You won't know until you track your expenses. We'll get into financial independence forecasting and calculations in later chapters, so don't worry too much about the 4% Rule. It's overly simplified, and I don't recommend relying on it solely for planning your life.

By tracking your expenses every year, you'll go from having no idea how your money is spent and no idea how much you need to achieve financial independence to consistently improving your spending habits and realizing you need far less than you think to be happy. You will hopefully realize that you don't need to work until you die.

Remember This:

- *The discipline to track your spending is the first step toward the discipline to stop spending.*
- *If you know your net worth but not how much you spend, you'll never accurately calculate your point of financial independence.*
- *Track your spending for three months alongside your net worth, and you'll see a similar change in your thinking.*

20. The dangers and opportunities of mortgages

The most significant purchases in your life will most likely be real estate. While real estate for rental income can be a productive investment, the vast majority of people will only purchase homes that they live in, which creates a different set of considerations financially. To simplify things just a bit, let's set aside the notion that a home you buy and live in is an investment. It will likely appreciate, that's true, but the other costs associated with buying, owning, and selling a home offset all the gains and then some. Buying a home is a lifestyle decision, not an investment decision. This doesn't mean you should make that decision frivolously or without analysis. Now if you find a killer deal, make the right improvements, and sell at the right time, you might very well make some profit. But probably not. Whether you own a home or plan to buy a home, it's better to look at the asset in terms of cost reduction, not future gains. You should be asking yourself, "How can I buy and maintain this home for as little as possible."

The first points to consider in buying a home aren't financial at all, although there is usually value created from them. Finding a home that has characteristics like the following is an important first consideration:

- Is it in a good school district?
- Is it in a safe area?
- Will you enjoy your desired lifestyle in the location?

If it meets those characteristics, the chances are that the house will also appreciate better than other properties. So now let's talk dollars. You'll need to figure out how much you can "afford" every month. This is not so that you can max out your disposable income! If you can afford a $1 million home scraping by paycheck to paycheck, try your hardest to find a home that meets your needs for half that. If you are constantly tapped out financially, you will miss exceptional opportunities to save money while you are paying an excessive amount in interest. This is the key to not only mortgages but all savings activities. Do not spend everything you have.

Down payments are a critical part of the equation for mortgages and almost all loans. It has become standard that a 20% down payment makes available to you the most favorable loans. Lower than 20% and you're considered risky. You'll even need special insurance, called Private Mortgage Insurance (PMI), which is a cost on top of the lender's interest rate. If you can't come up with a 20% down payment, hold off buying a home. Wait another year or two, and the money you'll save from PMI and higher interest rates will be substantial.

If you have more than 20%, you'll have to look at what other options you have for the money. You may want the psychological and emotional benefit of not owing to a bank money. Or perhaps you are heavy in the stock market and want to diversify your assets by putting more towards real estate. The choices are too specific to an individual's situation to describe in this chapter, but hopefully after reading this book, if you find yourself able to make a down payment greater than 20%, you'll also be able to evaluate your options.

Understanding the Tools You'll Need

Let's look at some math, and I'm going to use big, round numbers to help illustrate the points: The bank has approved you for that $1 million loan, but you've found a house that suits your needs for $500,000. Great! Conventional thinking says that you should get a 30-year mortgage because it gives you the lowest possible monthly bill. But since you could be paying for a $1 million, you have wiggle room and don't need to lowest possible payment. Remember, the lower the payment, the less you are paying towards the principal, which is paying back to yourself according to chapter 18 on net worth charts.

There are three keys to mortgages:

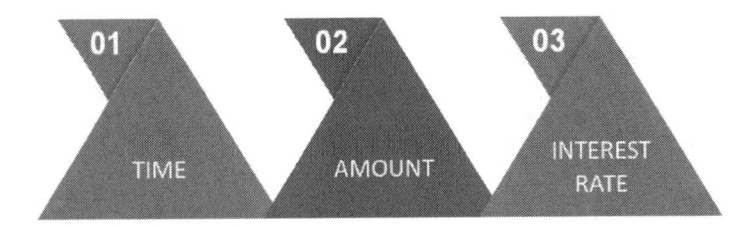

01 TIME
02 AMOUNT
03 INTEREST RATE

The higher these are, the more expense you'll incur over the life of the loan. You want:

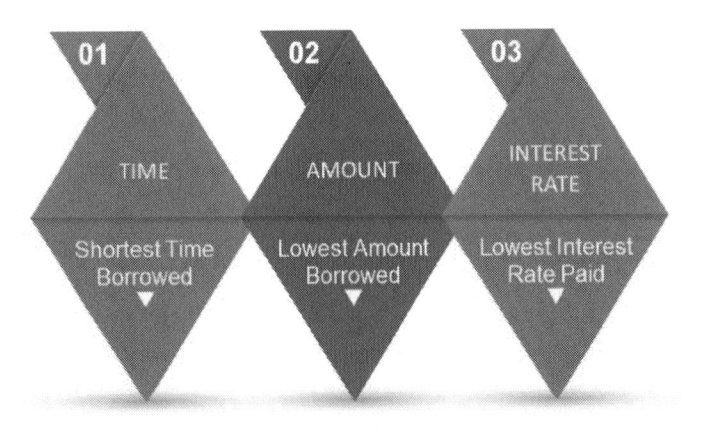

01 TIME — Shortest Time Borrowed ▼
02 AMOUNT — Lowest Amount Borrowed ▼
03 INTEREST RATE — Lowest Interest Rate Paid ▼

Your New Relationship With Money

Here's where most people stumble, and it's not their fault: the entire mortgage industry is built upon finding the highest possible earnings, which means convincing you to spend as much as possible. The way this typically happens is by making your monthly payments the lowest they can be. By spreading the amount over a long period, the monthly payment is less. Let's say you have a $100,000 loan at 0% interest for simplicity. If you have a 1-month loan, you owe all $100,000 after a month. If you have a 30-year mortgage, you owe $278 each month, which is $100,000 divided by 360 months. Attractive right?

Unfortunately, interest rates aren't 0%, so every month you carry a balance, you're paying interest. Each monthly payment will include interest and principal, which goes to lowering the balance. The principal should be viewed as savings because you are only moving it from your checking account into the equity of the house. On your net worth chart, it goes from one cell to another with no change.

A 30-year, $500,000 loan at 5% means that your first monthly payment is $2,684, with $601 of that being paid towards the principal. If you're keeping a net worth chart, this means your equity in the house increased $601 in a month.

Now let's look at a 15-year loan: with a shorter term, you'll get a better rate from the lender, so let's use 4.5%. Your monthly payment is now $3,825. That's $1,141 *more* a month, but that's ok because you have money to spare, remember? The big difference is that with this loan, you pay $1,950 back to yourself in that first month! And that number grows as you pay down the loan. So your out-of-

Understanding the Tools You'll Need

pocket increases $1,141, but your "savings" jumps a whopping $1,349.

	Interest Rate	Payment	1st Month Interest	1st Month Principal
30-Year	5.0%	$2,684	$2,083	$601
15-Year	4.5%	$3,825	$1,875	$1,950
Difference	0.5%	$1,141	($208)	$1,349

Let's look at the life of your loan: the first scenario of the 30-year loan has you paying $466,279 in interest over the life of the loan. The 15-year scenario has you paying only $188,494.

	Total Interest Paid
30-Year	$466,279
15-Year	$188,494
Difference	$277,785

Now if you had gone ahead and maxed yourself out on that $1 million home, after 30 years, you would have paid $932,558 in interest. If you assume that your life and enjoyment of both houses would be relatively the same, you've saved $744,064 by getting the less expensive home with the better mortgage. I use the expensive home to illustrate the point, but whether the difference in interest is $10,000 or $100,000 or $1 million, the savings are enormous. That's real money.

Your New Relationship With Money

Here are the two simple rules:

1. Don't spend the maximum amount which you can get loaned.
2. Use that difference in total house cost to get a loan that provides you with the most savings. Shorter lengths equal lower interest rates and higher monthly principal payoff.

If it is a safe home, provides a pleasant environment for your kids and makes you happy but is at the top end of your budget, it's probably still worth it to go ahead and buy it. Houses are long-term assets that have a tremendous impact on your quality of life. All I'm saying is that if you look for opportunities to save, chances are you'll find some great ones. If you're looking for opportunities to spend, there is no shortage of people looking to drain all your money.

What about refinancing? In short, don't bother unless you are <u>also</u> reducing the time left on the loan. If you're getting letters in the mail espousing the benefits of refinancing to a lower rate, the bank isn't doing it because it saves you money. If you're ten years into a mortgage and you refinance to a lower interest rate, you don't just save money. You get another 30-year mortgage, extending your total borrowing period to 40 years. If you want to save money on interest, just pay more principal every month. It won't save you money immediately, but over time it adds up. If you pay off an extra $1,000 one month, then each subsequent year you are saving the interest rate on that $1,000. It might only be $5 (5%), but that's $5 every year for the remaining time on the loan. If you put an extra $1,000 down a month, the impact starts to grow.

Understanding the Tools You'll Need

If you're looking at your mortgage and wondering how to manage it best, there are two scenarios I'd like to discuss:

1. Your interest rate is high, and lower rates are available.
2. Your interest rate is low, and a slightly lower rate is available.

If you're paying 5% and can now get 4.5%, you should refinance, but probably only to a shorter term. If you are five years into a 30-year mortgage, you should refinance to the lower rate and a new 15-year term. This means your total mortgage period will be only 20 years, a full decade less of paying interest. Please try to avoid 30-year loans.

If you fall into scenario 2, refinancing doesn't make a big difference in your total interest payments. You are better off merely reducing your loan by paying more of it off. There is a big assumption here: you have the money each month to pay an extra $50, $100, $250 towards your principal. If you don't have a little extra cash each month, it's probably time to evaluate your spending habits. Living below your means allows you to do things with money that others can't, such as paying down debt and saving significant amounts of money over the long-term.

Here are some examples of the math:

Let's use a 30-year, $300,000 mortgage with 25 years remaining, which means the balance is $275,947. If you did nothing and kept your 5% rate, you'd pay $279,767 in interest over 30 years. Refinanced to 4.5%, after 35 years (5 from the first loan, 30 from the next), you'd pay $299,133 in interest. That's right, you'd pay more because you already paid five years of substantial interest and are now extending your loan by another five years.

	Interest Rate	Years Active	Total Interest Paid
Original 30-Year	5.0%	5	$72,114
New 30-Year	4.5%	30	$227,019
Total		35	$299,133

Why would anyone do this? To lower their monthly bill! But in doing so, they'll pay more overall. It's a trap from mortgage lenders to make them money, not to benefit you. Now there is a possibility that interest rates have changed dramatically and you can get a rate low enough to make 35 years with the two loans less than the original loan, but you should do the math first.

Now if you pay $50 more a month to your 5% loan starting at year 25, you'd save almost $14,000. You avoided the whole headache of refinancing, shaved years off your term, and saved money! $100 more and you've saved $26,000. $500 more a month and you'll save $85,000 in interest. That's significant savings.

In summary, don't go searching for a lower monthly payment. You'll pay more over time to do so. If lower interest rates are available, you can refinance your mortgage, but it's likely only beneficial to do so only if you are getting a new term shorter than your remaining years. If you can squeeze a few bucks more out of your monthly budget and put it towards your mortgage, you'll save a lot of money. You'll also earn yourself months, years or perhaps a decade less of payments.

Buying a home is one of the largest and most serious purchases you'll make in life, so if there's ever a time to scrutinize the decision, this would be it. Borrowing costs aside, owning a home is expensive and not necessarily better than renting financially. You'll have repairs and taxes and utilities, all of which will eat a little bit out of your income. And once you have the home, the chances are that you'll eventually grow dissatisfied with some piece of it, leading to a most expensive activity: renovations…

Remember This:

- *Buying a home is a lifestyle decision, not an investment decision. But make that decision wisely.*

- *If you can't come up with a 20% down payment, hold off buying a home.*

- *Lower monthly payments equal more interest expense. Keep your terms short, even if you pay more per month.*

- *Mortgages are debt and are real expenses. Keep those expenses as low as possible.*

21. HGTV is distorting your reality

I love HGTV, let me admit that right off the bat. I love doing projects around the house and imagining all the cool things I can update. Home renovation projects, especially through the rose-colored lens of DIY TV shows, seem like can't lose situations. $5,000 for a bathroom? No problem! Except that bathroom renovations don't cost $5,000. They cost many multiples of that. Only on TV are things so fast and so reasonably priced.

So how much should you invest in a house? That's a pretty easy answer financially speaking, but the important thing to call out first is that having a home that you love has a profound effect on your life. Creating a space that makes you happy is an important thing. But it's easy to let it get out of hand, justifying extreme expenses with "I'll enjoy it," and it will create a "return on investment." The first thing to ask yourself isn't "will I enjoy it?" it should be, "could I enjoy the money more if I used it for something else?" $20,000 for a magnificent closet or $20,000 towards a magnificent vacation? Or towards an earlier retirement. Or college expenses. There's always an opportunity cost.

The second thing you should ask yourself is, "How much of this expense will I get back when I sell the house?" There is always a tipping point where you get less back on the final sale price of the house than what you put in. Make sure you have a realistic expectation of what a future buyer will pay for the work you're doing. Just because you decided to pay a certain amount for something doesn't mean a future buyer will do the same or pay more.

While the opportunity costs of putting money into a house are important, they are not unique to houses. You should be evaluating all expenses in terms of their opportunity costs. The real issue that sabotages homeowners' financial success with homes is assessing the return on investment.

Generally speaking, your house needs to be on par with the neighborhood. If you have a vintage 1970's bathroom and the neighborhood houses all have updates, if you invest just enough to make it contemporary and appealing, you can very easily create a positive return on investment. For example, $15,000 might get you a brand new bathroom and generate $30,000 in additional value in the house, because future buyers are willing to pay $15,000 more than it cost; they value not undergoing the hassle of a renovation. But a $50,000 bathroom might only get you $35,000 of extra value because the updates don't fit the neighborhood or buyers know they could have done it cheaper. And what's worse is if you already have an updated bathroom, but you don't like the style, your return on investment could be $0. The additional value you already paid for when you bought the house with a renovated bathroom, and the different design doesn't create anything more.

What almost always makes sense, if done reasonably, is an addition or creation of new space as long as the addition isn't grossly disproportionate to the comparable neighborhood houses. Bigger houses typically sell for more money, so creating new living space can add value to a house. Quick math would be to take an average cost per square foot of your neighborhood's houses and multiply that by the square feet you're adding. That's where the most return on investment happens. But again, it has to be done reasonably and in line with other houses. Adding 1,000 square feet of a bowling alley in your house is not the same as adding a bedroom.

Your New Relationship With Money

None of this provides a definitive answer to the original question, though. And that's like most complicated financial decisions: it's all relative to your personal situation. Here are some guiding principles to creating the best financial outcome through home renovations:

- Never spend more on a renovation where your purchase price of the house plus the renovation costs is higher than the comparable selling price in the neighborhood. And only consider renovating in this case when your lower purchase price was the result of unfinished or outdated spaces.
  - Example: The average home selling price is $300,000, and you paid $250,000 *solely* because the kitchen is a disaster. You should spend no more than $50,000 on this renovation.
- Avoid remodeling an already-updated, generally appealing space because it's not to your taste. Your return on investment could be $0.
  - Example: the previous owners remodeled the kitchen with new granite countertops. You prefer quartz. You've already paid for the value that was created in the additional remodel and therefore adding quartz doesn't create any more value than was already there.
- Consider additions to your home or the creation of new livable space if you have less square feet than the largest house in your neighborhood.
  - Example: Your house has 2,000 square feet, and the average house in your neighborhood is 2,000-2,500; building out unfinished attic space into a usable bonus room will typically create additional square feet and an additional value higher than the cost.

- Don't go into debt to renovate a home unless space is currently unusable. If you aren't going to sell it immediately, the interest you'll pay on the loan will outweigh the return generated with the renovation.

Real estate can make you some money, but don't get sucked into the traps of *renovation* = *ROI*. It's not that simple. That being said, don't be afraid to invest in your house. Whether the return is financial or emotional, if you do it wisely and understand the trade-offs, it's worth it.

Remember This:

- *Don't believe what you see on HGTV.*
- *Renovating already-updated spaces because it's not your specific taste creates little to no ROI.*
- *Don't invest more in your house where the purchase price plus renovation costs are more than the houses in your neighborhood are selling for.*
- *Don't add more debt on top of your mortgage to renovate.*

22. Relax, it's just taxes

I'm sorry to do this to you, but we have to talk about taxes. You don't need to be a tax expert in the end, but there are several fundamentals that are extremely important to learn. And remember that chapter on DIY? Managing and filing your own taxes falls under that category. With software like TurboTax, there's no reason to pay someone to do it; it's just not that hard, even if you consider yours "complicated." But this chapter isn't about filing taxes; it's about recognizing opportunities to avoid paying taxes. Let's be clear about the difference between evasion and avoidance: evasion is not paying when you are legally obligated. That's a crime. Avoidance is taking advantage of your 401k, making contributions to a Roth, and so on. Being smart about tax laws is a skill that has immediate and significant impacts.

First, a brief explanation of tax brackets: As your income goes up, the amount you pay in taxes goes up too, but there is some nuance to it. Your income is split into brackets, and each of those brackets is taxed at different rates. To explain it simply: let's say you have $1 of income. The government will take, for example, 10% of that dollar. If you have $2 of income, they'll take 10% of the first dollar and 15% of the next dollar. The third dollar will have 25% taken from it. Eventually, you'll have 37% taken out, and every dollar after that will also have 37% taken because that is the top bracket. As of writing this book in 2019, here are the federal income tax brackets for individuals and jointly-filing couples. This information

Understanding the Tools You'll Need

can also be found here: https://www.irs.gov/pub/irs-pdf/f1040es.pdf

Tax Rate	Single Filer	Married, Filing Jointly
10%	$0 to $9,700	$0 to $19,400
12%	$9,701 to $39,475	$19,401 to $78,950
22%	$39,476 to $84,200	$78,951 to $168,400
24%	$84,201 to $160,725	$168,401 to $321,450
32%	$160,726 to $204,100	$321,451 to $408,200
35%	$204,101 to $510,300	$408,201 to $612,350
37%	$510,301 and Up	$612,351 and Up

So if you are lucky enough to earn over $510,000 a year, don't think that you are paying 37% of <u>all</u> $510,000. What this does mean however is that as your income increases, you get to keep less of it. Going back to the $1 example, if each dollar takes you an hour to earn, then working 1 hour earns you $0.90 of take-home pay. But hour 3 provides you only $0.75, because you're taxed at 10% on the first dollar and 25% of the third dollar.

This does not mean that moving into a higher tax bracket results in you earning less. You're still taking home more and more money as you move up the brackets, you're just paying a higher amount of taxes for it.

And this is just federal income tax. There's also Social Security tax, Medicare tax, and State Income taxes. All of these are tacked on top. It adds up. Now understanding the differences between these other taxes aren't required to make good decisions, so we'll skip over them. Just know that they exist. Thinking strategically about your income, your investments, and the various benefits available to you can create tens of thousands and even hundreds of thousands of dollars in savings. Tax savings fall into two main categories:

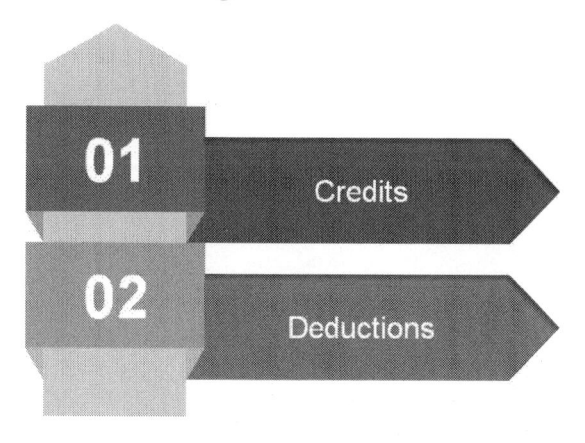

- 01 Credits
- 02 Deductions

Credits are actual dollar-for-dollar reductions in the taxes you owe. If you buy solar panels and get a $5,000 tax credit, for example, you'll pay $5,000 less in taxes. You may qualify for a Child Tax Credit or Earned Income Credit. These credits are typically pretty small because they are basically cashback from the government. Credits aren't that important relatively speaking, but it's important to understand the difference between them and the more important category of deductions. A deduction is something that reduces the amount of income that is taxable. If you earn $100,000 and have $10,000 in deductions, you are taxed only on $90,000. You don't save $10,000 like a tax credit; you save the 24% tax rate on that $10,000 (if you're a single filer). This example is

Understanding the Tools You'll Need

oversimplified because it doesn't factor in other taxes, but hopefully, it illustrates the point.

Tax deductions become more important as you climb the income ladder. In the same way that your money is worth less as your income goes up, the inverse applies to deductions: your deduction is worth more the higher your income. A $10,000 deduction in the 15% bracket is worth $1,500, but at the 37% bracket, it's worth $3,700. The more you earn, the more important it is that you master these deductions.

Without getting too far off-topic, the government gives you the option of taking a "Standard Deduction," which you can take instead of adding up all your donations, mortgage interest, and other deductions. In 2019, the Standard Deduction is $12,200 for single filers and $24,400 for jointly-filing married couples. If all your deductions add up to $10,000, you can instead take the standard deduction of $12,200 and benefit by the additional $2,200 the government is awarding you. But if your deductions total $15,000, you'll want to file your deductions and not take the government's standard deduction. The implication of the standard deduction is that only after your deductions have reached the standard deduction amount do they begin to provide any value.

For example, your mortgage interest only provides tax savings on what's above and beyond the standard deduction. You are getting the standard deduction no matter what, so it's as if nothing below $12,200 matters. If you have no deductions other than mortgage interest, for example, and that totals $15,000, the benefit of the deduction isn't on all $15,000, it's on the $2,800 above the standard deduction. If you're getting it anyway, you can't make spending decisions where you count the entire benefit.

One type of deduction that you're probably aware of is donations. When made to a legitimate charity, donations can reduce your taxable income. You can donate money, which is straight forward or you can donate stuff. Think of the tax deduction as income, because the item you're donating is a sunk cost and has no value to you anymore. If you can get even a few dollars back from the government, then that's a great deal. Determining the value of an item can be tricky, though. If you do your own taxes with Turbo Tax, there's a great feature which lets you search eBay for comparable items and use the IRS's "Sales of Comparable Properties" method for determining the value. It's straightforward and the "search" is automated and delivers a value back once you type in the name of your item. What this means is that you might be donating a video game that you originally bought for $60, and you now think it's worth $45; on eBay, they sell for $8. The IRS will let you deduct $8 of taxable income. At a 25% tax rate, you get back $2. That might not seem like a lot, but if you donate 50 articles of clothing, a couple of pieces of furniture, some electronics, a few books, etc., it can add up.

Don't mess with the IRS though. Over-valuation of items can lead to an audit, and you don't want that. So a designer purse might be "worth" $500 to you, but if it's selling on eBay for $50, it's worth $50 to the IRS. I recommend playing it safe and take the value Turbo Tax recommends. And donating items does some good for the world. If you can get $10 for the pants on eBay or give them to someone who needs them and get $2 back from the government as a thank you, perhaps just give them away.

The more impactful type of deduction is via savings tools such as a company-sponsored 401k or an IRA. You put money in, which is not taxed, and then it grows. We'll get to 401ks in the next chapter, but it's important to understand one more nuance of tax deductions, and that's the difference between tax-free grow and tax-deferred growth. A 401k isn't a permanent tax saving; it's simply deferring your tax payment into the future. When you withdraw it, you are taxed. Until that point, it grows, all the while postponing the tax bill. Tax-free growth, on the other hand, is precisely what it sounds like. A Roth IRA or Health Savings Accounts offer tax-free growth. Once the money is in the account, you never pay taxes on it. How and when you are allowed to take advantage of these tools is complicated, so we'll address that soon.

In the meantime, though, the government incentivizes you to save for retirement, donate to charity, and have children. Make sure you are aware of these incentives and maximize them. If you are committed to being a DIYer, there's no better way to learn about these incentives, then by filing your own taxes. And if you've adopted a net worth mindset, then forgoing money in your checking account for a larger amount in your 401k is a no brainer. Taxes are horrible and boring, and your eyes are probably glazing over finishing this chapter, but it's also imperative that you learn about them and make tax avoidance a cornerstone of your financial strategy.

Remember This:

- *Understanding the tax implications of your decisions will create some of the greatest returns in your life.*
- *Never pass on an opportunity from the IRS to defer or avoid taxes.*
- *Tax-Free and Tax-Deferred are different things.*

23. Traditional retirement savings plans

It's a popular mentality that "saving money" is solely the contributions to an IRA or 401k. Retirement savings accounts are just one of the many tools at your disposal, and to diverge from the conventional path, you need them all. And not only that, you need to max them all out. Retirement savings accounts can be categorized into the two main groups we discussed in the previous chapter on taxes:

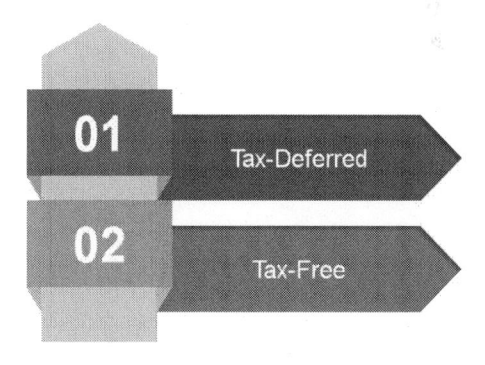

01 Tax-Deferred

02 Tax-Free

Understanding the Tools You'll Need

Tax-Deferred accounts include IRAs and 401ks. Tax-Free include Roth IRAs and Health Savings Accounts (HSA). Why is an HSA a "retirement account"? We'll get to that in a bit. Let's start with the most ubiquitous account type: the 401k.

The first thing to know about 401ks is that they are not your "nest egg." You probably can't retire on it alone. The other thing to know is that 401ks are nice gifts your company and your government give you. Most companies will match a certain amount, as in free money, and the government will defer the taxes you pay on that income until you start withdrawals at age 59 ½, when you'll hopefully and likely have a lower tax bracket. The company match and the tax-free compounding growth of this money are the keys. If you're getting a 100% match on 6% contributions (which is standard), that's like getting a 6% raise. That's an instant 100% return on investment. Beg, borrow or steal if you must, but don't skip this 6% contribution. Your paycheck goes down, I know. But your net worth should climb. Learn to live off less money and experience the benefit of free company money and fewer taxes. After 6%, you're not getting a match from your employer, but the government still lets you make tax-deferred contributions up to the limit. As of writing this book in 2019, the IRS limit is $19,000. Make that your goal.

If you don't have a company-sponsored 401k, you can open up an individual IRA with a brokerage firm. You'll have to make contributions with after-tax dollars, but come tax time, you will get that deduction benefit. Personal IRAs provide no matching contribution, and the limit is lower, $6,000 a year, but you should still have one if you don't have a 401k.

When you begin to make withdrawals at age 59.5, which is the minimum age to do so without penalty, those withdrawals are treated as income. That income is all taxable in the same way your income today is. If the percent you pay in taxes at the time of withdrawal is the same that you were paying when the contribution was made, there is no tax benefit. And if you are earning more in retirement than you did while you were making those contributions, you'll pay more in taxes. In these scenarios, the 401k has served simply as a savings tool, and your gain has been the company match. However, if your tax rate is lower in retirement, which is likely, you'll realize the additional benefit of lower taxes being paid.

Moving on to tax-free accounts, the Roth IRA is a really powerful tool. So powerful in fact that the government limits annual contributions to $6,000 (as of 2019) and also prevents people over a certain income level to participate. For individuals, that income level is $122,000 when your contribution amount is reduced, and you're fully ineligible at $137,000. For married, filing jointly, the income level is $193,000 and the household is fully ineligible at $203,000.

Tax Rate	Contributions are Phased Out	Ineligible
Single	$122,000	$137,000+
Married, Filing Jointly	$193,000	$203,000+

Understanding the Tools You'll Need

Because of this, it's even more important to contribute to a Roth as early and as fully as you can. When money goes into a Roth, it's after-tax, so there's no deduction, but once it goes in, you never pay taxes again. If your $6,000 contribution grows to $10 million, you owe the government nothing. The longer your money sits, the more it grows. And it's all tax-free. And this becomes important when you are forecasting your retirement income and trying to estimate your tax burden. With the Roth, there's no tax burden. You withdraw what you need to spend.

The other valuable tax-free account is the Health Savings Account (HSA). The idea is that the government is giving you a tax break on what is, essentially, your deductible for an insurance plan. Most people with a high deductible insurance plan will go through the IRS contribution limit of $3,500 a year in medical expenses I imagine. For families, the limit if $7,000 allowed by the IRS. A crucial caveat to the HSA: You must have a "high deductible" insurance plan as determined by the IRS, which is at least $1,350 for a single person and $2,700 for a family plan. And also don't get the HSA mixed up with the FSA, the Flexible Spending Account, for low-deductible plans. The FSA is a use-it-or-lose-it plan that doesn't roll over your funds.

If you have company-provided health insurance, the chances are that you've been offered one or both of these savings plans. You are probably also confused about the differences. Both Health Savings Accounts and Flexible Spending Accounts allow you to deduct income from your taxes and then spend that money on qualified medical expenses. Within reason, almost everything is qualified:

hospital visits, medication, eye exams, etc. Things like teeth whitening, nutritional supplements like protein powder, or anything that results in aesthetic improvements are not qualified. But it's all gray. If your doctor says, "whitening your teeth will improve X condition," it's qualified.

An HSA is essentially another 401k, which is incredible, and why it's included in this retirement savings section. You'll spend a lot of it on normal medical expenses, but you'll have the instant tax benefit on that money you put in. And if you don't spend it, you can earn a tax-free return when it's invested. At 65, you can pull it out for whatever reason (and pay taxes on the income then). You should look to max out your HSA contributions every year you are eligible to do so. You may phase-out of Roth eligibility, but the HSA will always be available as long as you have a high deductible medical plan.

Your mentality toward retirement savings plans should be to maximize every opportunity. With your net worth mindset, the money is always with you, right on the page. You'll be capitalizing on tax benefits and company matches while investing and growing your money. Before you think about buying a rental property, investing in cryptocurrencies or bankrolling a trip to Vegas, max out your available retirement plans. Treat the remainder as your real income, which can be disruptive and painful early on, but also impactful. You will need to balance the desire for baby steps with the discouraging feeling of not making progress. Consider a dramatic change. And do it with these retirement plans.

Understanding the Tools You'll Need

Plan	Contribution Limit
401k	$19,000
Roth IRA	$6,000
Traditional IRA	$6,000
Health Savings Account	$3,500/$7,500

Remember This:

- *Avoid baby steps in retirement plan contributions. The earlier you max them out, the better.*
- *Contribute to your 401k at the full amount that is matched (6%), and then also contribute up to the IRS max of $19,000.*
- *Don't miss an opportunity to contribute to a Roth IRA*
- *Always contribute to a Health Savings Account.*
- *Max. Them. Out.*

24. Credit and large purchases

You've probably heard the term "good debt" before, but the chances are that you were being marketed to at the time, likely without knowing it. There are all kinds of debt, also known as credit, available to Americans, and those offering this money want nothing more than you to take on as much debt as you possibly can (and then some). There are a bunch of different interpretations and classifications of good vs. bad debt, so I'll just run through my personal opinions on the matter.

In the most general terms: Good debt means the loaning of money that creates an opportunity for you to make more money. This is called "leverage" in investing terms. Bad debt is the loaning of money that creates no incremental value and ends up costing more than the original cost.

Good debt isn't something that many people will come across except a mortgage, and even then, it's a little gray. Putting 4% down on a 30-year loan is not good debt. Yes, you'll earn money as the house appreciates, but you are spending an extraordinary amount in interest, and you won't recoup those costs. 20% down on a 15-year loan and the money you'll make on real estate appreciation will likely outweigh the interest payments. But you might have significant repairs and other expenses associated with the maintenance and the sale of the house that eat up this benefit. You won't get rich buying and living in homes. And as a result, mortgages lean towards bad debt, not good debt. Let's call it "not so bad, reasonably acceptable debt."

Understanding the Tools You'll Need

Good debt would be the bank loaning you money at 3% and you taking that sum, investing it in something and earning more than 3%. Many brokerage firms offer margin accounts where you can borrow money like this and invest it. Business loans would also be a good example, using a loan to start a business that generates more money. If you are confident in your investment opportunity, good debt can be a really powerful tool.

Another important characteristic of good debt is if you already have the money. Confused? Going back to the example above of earning a greater return than that of the interest rate: if you have $200,000 in a brokerage account earning 8% and want to purchase a rental property that costs $200,000, you could either pay cash or get a loan. If your loan is for 3%, then you are much better off keeping your cash where it is and getting the loan.

Leverage works both ways though: if you borrow money, invest in something and that something declines, then not only do you owe the money back with interest, but you have less than what you borrowed. Leverage is a powerful tool, but it can be powerful destructive as well, so consider it carefully.

Leverage and good debt do not apply to most purchases, though. If you have $1,000 in cash and want to buy a $1,000 washing machine, it is not good debt to finance it. Why? Because it's entirely impractical to invest that $1,000 and earn a good return. Remember, in month zero, you have $1,000 earning a return, but in month one, it's $950 since you had to make a payment on your loan. Each time you do this, you need to pay a fee to purchase an investment. Practically speaking, loans for consumer goods can never be justified by keeping equivalent cash in the market. Additionally, washing machines don't appreciate. You are borrowing money to buy something that loses value over time. Just pay the $1,000 for the washing machine if you really need it.

Most credit is bad debt. If you don't have the money to buy something and that something depreciates, any credit you use to buy it is bad debt. 0% financing is bad debt. If a company can offer you 0% financing, they are screwing you some other way. If you don't pay it off in time, you will get killed by the eventual interest rate, for example. Or, the price you are paying for the item is inflated.

If you don't have a $1,000 for that washing machine, you shouldn't buy it. Plain and simple. If you don't have $30,000 for that car, don't consider buying it. A $60,000 car at 0% might be an efficient use of debt if it weren't a car, which depreciates. You don't need to spend that much. So for cars, you shouldn't spend so much on a vehicle where you could earn a good return over time on the cash. 0% is a marketing ploy, and like all marketing ploys, the result is that you are separated from more money than you otherwise would have been. This isn't to say that if you have the cash, you *should* buy something. If you don't have the cash, don't even consider it. And if you do have the cash, do some due diligence in making that decision.

Except for mortgages, education, care for your children or health emergencies, and maybe a few other corner cases, you shouldn't finance anything. Hold onto your money until you can afford to pay in cash. When it comes time for really big loans, having no other debt will save you a ton of money.

Debt helps create growth. It's a primary component of every economy in the world. Unfortunately, it's also a tool for people to live outside their means. So be careful with your debt. If used wisely, you can create tremendous value. If handled poorly, it can ruin you.

Remember This:

- *Good debt creates more value than the cost. Bad debt costs you more.*
- *0% interest is still bad for consumer purchases.*
- *"I'm earning more in the market" is a poor justification for financing a purchase.*

25. Don't hide cash under your mattress

Perhaps the most controversial advice in this book will be this: forget your concept of an emergency fund. I see a lot of people who carry 6 or 12 months of living expenses around in cash, and I think that's a mistake. There's this old fashion concept that keeping your money in the "bank," also known as a checking account is the most responsible thing to do. I disagree. With all of the pre-tax and post-tax investment tools available, the least productive thing you can do is take your income, pay taxes, and then let it sit in cash. Over time it will be worth less and less due to inflation. A checking account has no real opportunities for return. Checking accounts hold your money hostage. That's why I recommend a minimum cash balance concept. This is not the minimum needed to have an account which is typically around $500; this is the minimum you need to pay all your bills.

But what about emergencies! Don't get me wrong, you need access to money for emergencies and a year's worth of living expenses is a good goal. But you don't need that money under your mattress. Or a checking account. It can be both doing something and be available on short notice. So keep enough cash on hand to meet the 24-hour needs, but then invest the rest in a brokerage account. If an emergency arises, which is rare by its very nature, you can sell whatever you need. Perhaps you'll sell with a gain, perhaps with a loss, but again, it's for rare occasions.

Back to the minimum cash balance concept: Think of your checking account as a holding ground for monthly payments to your credit cards, utility bills, and mortgage payments. Keep enough cash in your checking account to pay these bills and then move the rest into a brokerage or investment account. If you're participating in a retirement plan through work, you can also open up a personal investment account with the same company to keep things simple. You can initiate transfers to and from your brokerage account for free and very quickly. So if you're a bit short in your checking for a particular month, transfer some money. Again, it's free. And by the way, you can likely use your brokerage account just like a bank account, so don't think of the cash as being restricted there.

Understanding the Tools You'll Need

The key to making this work is your net worth chart. If you don't have one, it's going to be much harder to execute this cleanly while avoiding any overdrafts. The steps are easy:

- Make sure your paychecks are direct-deposited into your checking account.
- Make sure all your bills are paid from checking as well.
- Proactively pay off larger bills like credit cards before the new statement is generated. This gives you time to adjust your cash balance if need be.
- Move the surplus cash into your brokerage account. If your monthly bills are $3,000 and you like to have a buffer of $1,000 in checking, move everything over $4,000 into the other account.

What's the point of all this? Simple: keep your money where you have an opportunity to earn a return. It might not seem like a big deal if you're moving $50 a month to your brokerage account, but what if that was $500 a month. Or $5,000? Like everything else, return on investment adds up. Get in the habit of keeping your money "working." If it's not a huge payoff for you today, it will be later in life, so develop the right habits.

Remember This:

- *Forget your concept of an emergency fund and keep your money working.*
- *Keep enough cash in your checking account to pay your recurring bills and then move the rest into a brokerage or investment account.*

26. The art of negotiating

Everything I know about negotiating I learned on Kho San Road in Bangkok, Thailand. If you've seen the Leo DiCaprio movie "The Beach," you might remember the opening scene where Richard drinks the snake blood—that's Kho San Road. Or at least it's supposed to be. It's a backpacker's haven and an enjoyable place.

When I first visited Thailand, I stayed a block away from Kho San Road and spent quite a bit of time exploring the area. You can find anything you need, and nothing has a price tag. Show up clueless, and you'll pay $5 for a t-shirt. Haggle a bit, and you'll get 2 for $1. At first, negotiating was awkward. I didn't feel comfortable asking a nice Thai lady for her "best price." But after a while, I grew to love it. It's part of the culture, and after a few lengthy negotiations the shop owners would shake my hand, and we'd part, deal complete.

So what did I learn about negotiation techniques, and how does it apply to life in the US? Here's a normal progression:

Understanding the Tools You'll Need

1. If you are looking for the lowest price, never be the one to make the first offer. This is different from salary negotiations by the way, just FYI.
2. Act surprised by the first price. You can also try shocked.
3. Counter with a low ball, try 50% of the asking price.
4. Bring up the competition. On Kho San Road, there are 100 places to buy jade elephants, so let them know that you know they aren't the only shop in town.
5. Counter again with a sizable bump, but still a low ball.
6. Say no thanks and start to walk away.
7. Let them call you back.
8. Counter again with a smaller bump. If you want, declare it to be your final offer.
9. Say no thanks and start to walk away.
10. Make your final offer.

It's important to be friendly but matter-of-fact. Wear sunglasses if you think you'll have trouble playing the part. And be sure to know the market; shop around and gauge prices before you get into negotiations. The real key to negotiations is creating a situation where you have leverage. If you are a single buyer with multiple sellers and you are willing to walk away, you will win. The walking away is the tough part. If you go into negotiations knowing that you have to make the purchase, you will likely lose out on a deal.

House purchases work the same way even though the stakes are higher. And yes, I'm aware that this is simplifying a very complicated, emotional and stressful process:

1. Make a lowball offer that shows you're serious and doesn't offend the seller. (Offering $100,000 for a $500,000 asking price will immediately and permanently end the discussion.)
2. Let the seller counter with a reduction.
3. Counter with a sizable bump that shows you are willing to play ball.
4. Seller counters again.
5. A little more back and forth with smaller and smaller adjustments.
6. Say no thanks and walk away.
7. Wait for another offer the seller or come back at a later time with an increase, a favorable term like fast close period and some comparable sales data to show that you're knowledgeable and ready to make a deal. Perhaps make this your final offer.
8. Work out the details in a way favorable to the seller to allow him or her to save face and close on a great deal.

Negotiating can be uncomfortable, but you'll need this skill. You might not find many opportunities to negotiate purchases, but you'll have the chance to negotiate compensation at a job. The stakes are a little higher when negotiating salary, but the principals are the same:

- Know your value.
- Know the value other like-companies are paying for similar roles.
- Create some leverage by working on multiple opportunities.

Understanding the Tools You'll Need

- Counter effectively.
- Don't be afraid to walk away.

These are skills and require some practice and a lot of confidence. So if you are visiting a country where haggling is part of the culture, give it a run. Saving 50 cents on a t-shirt might teach you the lessons you'll need to save $50,000 on the house or make $50,000 more at your next job. And if you find haggling in a poor country distasteful, you can always win the negotiation and give them more.

Remember This:

- *Negotiating is a valuable skill in a variety of situations, including life's most important financial decisions.*
- *Know the true value of what you are negotiating over.*
- *Don't be afraid to walk away.*

27. Investing for growth

Investing is tough. The only reason every person isn't a total failure is that over time, markets grow. Take a look at this graph. It's the S&P 500 index since 1928. So if you invest your money broadly, also known as diversification, and keep it long enough, you'll make money. That's the nature of modern economies. I would be remiss if I didn't also point out that advanced economies will also suffer recessions and depressions after periods of growth. You can see those dips in the graph as well.

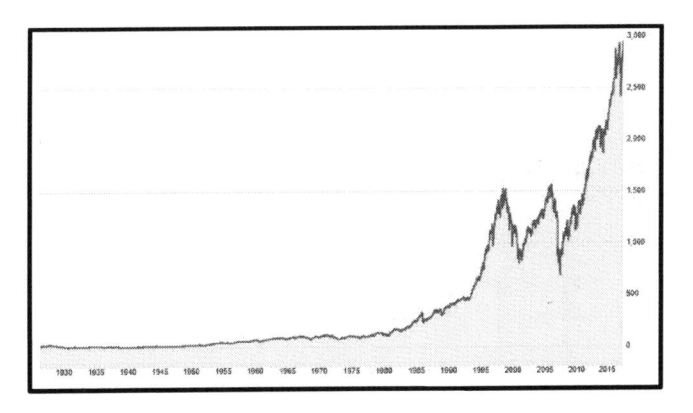

So if markets go up, why isn't everyone rich? Well, there are two reasons:

1. If you "wait out" the market, you'll also wait out a good bit of growth and only earn a modest return.
2. If you try to beat the market, you'll most likely fall victim to any number of dangerous emotional investing pitfalls.

Let's ignore the financial aspects of investing for a moment and think about the following dangers. Your gut

Understanding the Tools You'll Need

will tell one thing, and it will be wrong. Trust that fact. Here are some ideas to stew over:

- If you hear about a "great idea," then you've already missed out. Thousands upon thousands of professional investors have heard about the idea months ago, made their money, and moved on.
- When you're scared that the market might never recover, invest more. Look at the graphs above. See the recessions? Imagine if you would have invested when the media was shouting "depression!" and you were worried about losing your job.
- When you think the market is unstoppable, consider trimming back your exposure. Remember right before the 2008 recession when real estate could never fail, and the market was growing by leaps and bounds? Or what about the dot-com boom? Collect some or all of your winnings and sit it out. It will go down and then rebound.
- Don't try to "beat" anything. "Beating" = "Gambling." Think you have a "can't lose" idea? See above bullets.

Investing is as much about making money as it is not losing it. Keep these things in mind next time you're investing. Investing is part discipline and part good decision making. When it comes to discipline, you have to resist the urge to check your investments every day. You'll drive yourself insane watching your account drop or grow $1, or $100 or $1,000 in a day. It is hard to not get emotional about investments and experience anxiety. Just try not to get too excited if you make a lot and please don't feel bad if you lose it. If you've made sound long-term investments, the bumps in the road will all smooth out.

So what exactly is a stock? And what does it mean to buy one? Without derailing the entire book on the complexities of the stock market, of which I am far from an expert anyway, let's simplify: Whether you have an account with Fidelity, Vanguard, Charles Schwab, E-Trade or a private investment firm, what you are buying is a small piece of another company and expecting it to grow in value. Look at your house, for example, and take 1% of its $500,000 value. We'll call that a share, and it's valued at $5,000. Fast forward a year, and your house is now valued at $550,000; your share is worth $5,500. You could sell that share to someone else for $5,500 because that buyer thinks it will be worth $6,000 in another year. Buying a share of a company is essentially the same thing, except the markets move based on expectations of future values, not current values. If news comes out that a company has developed a killer new product, its stock price will likely go up. And the opposite will happen if a product fails.

You can buy shares of individual companies or baskets of shares from multiple companies. These come in the form of Exchange Traded Funds (ETF) and Mutual Funds. ETFs are the more basic of the two, comprised of a set of stocks that sit there and move as the market. An ETF could be 25% Apple shares, 25% Google, 25% Microsoft, and 25% Amazon; the price of that ETF share moves around with the weighted value of those stocks. A Mutual Fund is managed, meaning that there is an investor behind the scenes making trades, buying, selling, and generally looking to make the most money.

Understanding the Tools You'll Need

If you're new to investing, stick with ETFs. You can purchase shares of a "Total Market" ETF, meaning it will move in value relative to the entire stock market. Or you can get an ETF that's only Tech stocks, or High Growth companies, Real Estate, Medical Supplies, etc. But what to choose? Pick something you feel confident in the long term. Do you believe that Energy companies in the US will continue to grow? Or do you think that Telecom companies are a stable bet over the next ten years? You'll need to do some research. Look at the historical returns. Has the valued climbed steadily over the past 20 years? How much did it drop during the last recession? Compare these answers to the ETFs you are considering, and you'll start to get an idea of what you have the most confidence in. But whatever you do, don't put a lot of money into what you think is the "next big thing." An experimental amount you are willing to lose is ok, but don't go all in hoping to strike it big.

One specific thing to highlight is dividends. If you learn nothing else about stocks, understand dividends. Some companies use dividend payments to entice investors: each quarter the company will announce that each share gets a certain amount of money. A $50 share might get $0.50 paid to the investor, which can be used (automatically if you want) to buy more shares. The next quarter you'll get another $0.50, and after four quarters, you have been paid $2 for holding that stock. $2 divided by $50 is a 4% dividend. Large companies with consistent performance can pay reliable dividends. So even if the stock price is jumping around, you're getting that $2 every year (for example). Over time, this is a really big deal. A stock with no growth in share price can still be a valuable investment due to compounding growth. A 4% dividend, reinvested each quarter, is a good, stable investment for your portfolio. This is why dividends exist.

The first topic you'll come across when researching investments is "diversification." The idea is simply that within the stock market as a whole, some investments go up, while others go down. If you have too much exposure to a single investment, you could strike it big, or you could go broke. Everybody has their advice on diversification, whether it be stocks and bonds, or overseas and domestic, or by way of multiple industries. Your level of risk tolerance will dictate where you put your money, but I will say that if you have aggressive plans for financial independence, you'll need aggressive investing and that comes with some risk. As long as you aren't betting on Hail Marys, you can find good growth opportunities with minimal risk. We're not talking 100% annual returns, but good enough returns to make a difference in your financial wellbeing. Consider finding ETFs that are spread across several stocks that fit a profile you believe in such as consistent dividend payers, utilities, natural resources, technology, etc.

The stock market is dynamic, complex, and overwhelming. But it's also an absolute requirement to be a part of if you want to grow your wealth. An hour of research can yield great knowledge. You also may grow to love the challenge of investing. If your palms are sweaty reading this chapter, then buy an "S&P 500 ETF" and call it a day. Over the next decades, you'll do fine.

Understanding the Tools You'll Need

Remember This:

- *If you want to be financially independent, you need to be investing.*
- *Never, ever listen to your gut when making investment decisions. Do the opposite.*
- *Focus on ETFs in industries you believe are stable.*
- *Take advantage of dividends.*
- *Earning a positive return is not a guarantee. Be prepared to lose money on some investments.*

Part 4
Putting It Into Action

28. You can do this

Here we go.

Hopefully, by now, you understand why the game plan for your financial independence comes last. Without a purpose and a set of clearly defined goals, there's nothing to achieve. And even if you have a clear vision for your life, without understanding the tools, techniques, pitfalls, and opportunities, you'll run around in circles. To be successful, you need both a destination and a means to get there. Now you can start the journey.

A little self-reflection is always beneficial and especially now that we're getting into the tactical components of this relationship with money. I encourage you to take a few minutes and document your biggest aha learnings in the first three chapters as well as the goals that might have come to mind as you've read.

Your New Relationship With Money

Biggest Aha Learnings	Personal Goals

Putting It Into Action

It's important to understand that addressing one of the activities in this last section of the book isn't good enough. Creating a net worth chart every month, but neglecting to participate in your company's 401k plan won't do you much good. Conversely, saving as much money as you can, but not tracking and investing it effectively won't yield very good returns. All of the following chapters and action items are pieces to a larger puzzle. Each one might only provide a few hundred dollars of benefit at first, but over time, they'll grow. As your income increases, as your investments improve, as your lifestyle changes, so too, will your financial situation become stronger. This is as much about discipline as it is about knowledge and planning.

I encourage you to be disciplined about each chapter at first. Some will be harder than others, but the *discipline* to do what is easy will help motivate you to tackle those tasks that are painful. Over time you may decide that you no longer need to be as regimented in certain areas and that's fine. The training wheels can come off eventually. But don't stop pedaling.

Here we go.

29. Your net worth chart

The very first thing you need to do is create your net worth chart. Read this chapter, put the book down, create your chart, and then come back. If you haven't picked on this yet, the net worth chart is the fundamental tool for changing both your relationship with money and your strategy for managing it. I really can't stress its importance enough. Tracking your net worth can show you, at the very highest level, if you are living above or below your means. It shows you how much you are saving or how much you need to cut from your expenses. It shows you when you are financially independent. It shows everything.

What's the date today? Let's make this day the day each month you update this chart. Once you start tracking all the components that make up your financial life, just focusing on one total number month over month isn't the most effective way to monitor your finances. You also need to calculate and track categories within the total, as well as the components of each category. Once your net worth is compartmentalized, you can more easily analyze the results. Consider tracking these categories and accounts first:

Retirement Assets:

- 401k
- Roth IRA
- Pension
- Health Savings Account

Non-Retirement Assets:

- Checking Account
- Brokerage/Investment Account
- 529 College Savings Plan
- Deferred Income Plans
- Company Stock Plans

Real Estate:

- House Value
- Mortgage Balance

Short Term Liabilities:

- Credit Card Debt
- Car Loans
- Student Loans

Other Assets:

- Cars
- Jewelry
- Art
- Other Valuables and Collectibles

You can start to see that having categories allows you to understand the results of your monthly net worth chart very easily. Let's use retirement accounts as our demonstration and keep in mind that the numbers are just placeholders. In Excel, start building out these sections on one tab:

Your New Relationship With Money

Retirement Accounts					$35K
401k	**$20K**	**Pension**	**$9K**	**Roth IRA**	**$4K**
Large Cap ETF	$5K	Cash Balance	$5K	Large Cap ETF	$1K
Small Cap ETF	$5K			Small Cap ETF	$1K
Dividend ETF	$5K	**Health Savings Account**	**$2K**	Dividend ETF	$1K
S&P 500 ETF	$5K	Cash Balance	$2K	S&P 500 ETF	$1K

List out each account and each investment. The numbers in bold are the sum of the parts for each account. It's important to track each investment because while your total account value might climb, some investments will underperform. You will be able to identify those and make changes. If you only track the total, you'll never know how the individual components are performing over time.

Now set up your taxable investment accounts and cash accounts:

Non-Retirement Assets					$39K
Brokerage Account	**$12K**	**Checking Account**	**$10K**	**529 Plan**	**$8K**
Large Cap ETF	$3K	Cash Balance	$10K	Large Cap ETF	$8K
Small Cap ETF	$3K				
Dividend ETF	$3K	**Deferred Income Plan**	**$3K**	**Company Stock Plan**	**$6K**
S&P 500 ETF	$3K	Cash Balance	$3K	Shares	$6K

I like to have real estate be a separate category, with both the asset and the liability (mortgage) shown:

Real Estate				$100K
Home	**$300K**	**Mortgage**	**($200K)**	
Market Value	$300K	Remaining Balance	($200K)	

And liabilities such as student loans, credit cards, and car payments:

Short-Term Liabilities					($73K)
Credit Cards	**($2K)**	**Car Loans**	**($21K)**	**Student Loans**	**($50K)**
Visa	($1K)	Car 1	($10K)	Remaining Balance	($50K)
Mastercard	($1K)	Car 2	($11K)		

Lastly, your other assets:

Putting It Into Action

Other Assets				$27K
Cars	$27K	Other	$4K	
Car 1	$12K	Jewelry	$2K	
Car 2	$15K	Art	$2K	
		Other	$1K	

Now total it all up, and you have your chart. Once you have these categories and their components, you can also summarize the detail into useful numbers like cash investments and available cash:

TOTAL NET WORTH	$129K
Retirement	$35K
Cash Investments	$20K
Available Cash	$10K

Save this file and create a new tab for next month.

Retirement Accounts					$35K
401k	$20K	Pension	$9K	Roth IRA	$4K
Large Cap ETF	$5K	Cash Balance	$5K	Large Cap ETF	$1K
Small Cap ETF	$5K			Small Cap ETF	$1K
Dividend ETF	$5K	Health Savings Account	$2K	Dividend ETF	$1K
S&P 500 ETF	$5K	Cash Balance	$2K	S&P 500 ETF	$1K

Non-Retirement Assets					$39K
Brokerage Account	$12K	Checking Account	$10K	529 Plan	$8K
Large Cap ETF	$3K	Cash Balance	$10K	Large Cap ETF	$8K
Small Cap ETF	$3K				
Dividend ETF	$3K	Deferred Income Plan	$3K	Company Stock Plan	$6K
S&P 500 ETF	$3K	Cash Balance	$3K	Shares	$6K

Real Estate				$100K
Home	$300K	Mortgage	($200K)	
Market Value	$300K	Remaining Balance	($200K)	

Short-Term Liabilities					($73K)
Credit Cards	($2K)	Car Loans	($21K)	Student Loans	($50K)
Visa	($1K)	Car 1	($10K)	Remaining Balance	($50K)
Mastercard	($1K)	Car 2	($11K)		

Other Assets				$27K
Cars	$27K	Other	$4K	
Car 1	$12K	Jewelry	$2K	
Car 2	$15K	Art	$2K	
		Other	$1K	

TOTAL NET WORTH	$129K
Retirement	$35K
Cash Investments	$20K
Available Cash	$10K

Once you have two months, look at them side-by-side. What changed? Did your net worth increase or decrease? Did automatic retirement savings contributions drive it? Or did your spending bring it down? You'll be able to answer these questions now. Knowing is half the battle. Not only will you be smarter about your money when you lay it all out there but slowly your mentality will start to change. When a 401k contribution shows up in the Retirement box instead of the Cash box, it doesn't feel like a loss.

However you want to construct the net worth chart is going to be fine, as long as you capture everything and it's realistic and accurate. You might not like viewing numbers in the way I've designed this example, and that's perfectly ok. You're the only one who's going to see this chart, so make it something that you want to come back to each month.

Come back to it, though. It's the essential part of this new relationship with money.

Remember This:

- *Break your net worth chart into broad categories.*
- *Track each investment within each account.*
- *There's no right or wrong design as long as all the detail is captured and accurate.*
- *Do it every month.*

30. Net worth goal setting

So let's set some goals. How much did your net worth increase after one month? $100? $1,000? $10,000? And how much is that as a percentage of the total? When your net worth is low, a small gain can be a large percentage. Over time, hitting that same percentage becomes more difficult. To start the goal-setting process, take your first month's or two month's percentage change, multiply it by 12, add a little bit on top and there you go. If you grew 1%, then perhaps 12% for the year is on track, so make it 15%. Adjust your goals over time to continually outpace your standard growth rate. Depending on where you are at in your life and also how long you've been focused on net worth growth, your goals will be different.

I should caveat the goal-setting objective: total growth might not always be the best approach. Depending on your long term goals, you'll need to consider cash flow, accessibility of funds from retirement accounts, liquidity vs. real estate, and other factors. You might have $10 million of real estate sitting around, but no income and no cash. That won't help you much unless you start selling properties. That being said, the pursuit of net worth growth will sort itself out. The government will only let you save so much in retirement accounts each year; your paycheck will only be so big, your accessibility to mortgages to buy real estate will have limits. For the majority of your working life, simply focusing on net worth growth is the best advice I can give. Once you determine a specific plan for your life and your retirement, you can focus your attention on specific areas.

Your New Relationship With Money

In the end, your net worth is the value of everything you own. Some money might be more challenging to access than others, but it's all there and all yours. Once you reach 60, most, if not all, of the money across your portfolio will become available to you penalty-free. Unless you plan to stop working very early, you won't need to balance short term cash needs before your retirement accounts become available. Regardless of your plans for work and income, you want as much as possible so that you can achieve your purpose.

When your financial goal is as holistic as net worth growth, you begin to see things differently. Having a lot of cash on hand might have felt good a while ago, but now, it hinders your ability to grow your net worth. Putting money into a Health Savings Account might have been the least exciting thing you could imagine, but now it's an easy way to save on taxes and bump that net worth number higher.

Looking back to Chapter 14, I discussed the value in understanding your spending and shared the following chart:

Putting It Into Action

Savings Rate	Years of Financial Independence	Years Needed to Save 1 Year of Expenses
5%	0.05	19.00
10%	0.11	9.00
15%	0.18	5.67
20%	0.25	4.00
25%	0.33	3.00
30%	0.43	2.33
35%	0.54	1.86
40%	0.67	1.50
45%	0.82	1.22
50%	1.00	1.00
55%	1.22	0.82
60%	1.50	0.67
65%	1.86	0.54
70%	2.33	0.43
75%	3.00	0.33
80%	4.00	0.25
85%	5.67	0.18
90%	9.00	0.11
95%	19.00	0.05

Understanding your saving rate is incredibly valuable, but in the end, what matters is your net worth. The goal you set to grow should also be viewed through the lens of how much spending it covers. If your net worth grows $10,000 in a year and that's a 5% increase on $200,000, but you spend $100,000 a year, you'll need ten years to grow enough not to work one year.

Your New Relationship With Money

$200,000 Net Worth. $100,000 Annual Expenses

Net Worth Growth %	Net Worth Growth $	Years of Financial Independence
5%	$10,000	0.10
10%	$20,000	0.20
15%	$30,000	0.30
20%	$40,000	0.40
25%	$50,000	0.50
30%	$60,000	0.60
35%	$70,000	0.70
40%	$80,000	0.80
45%	$90,000	0.90
50%	$100,000	1.00
55%	$110,000	1.10
60%	$120,000	1.20
65%	$130,000	1.30
70%	$140,000	1.40
75%	$150,000	1.50
80%	$160,000	1.60
85%	$170,000	1.70
90%	$180,000	1.80
95%	$190,000	1.90

This is overly simplified, I know, but the principle is important. Each year, your net worth will hopefully grow, and those percentages will represent larger and larger dollar amounts. Don't get discouraged if you are far from growing your net worth a substantial amount, but also don't lose sight of the fact that you must get there.

Putting It Into Action

Remember the Future Value Excel calculations we did? Take a moment to do a test run on your current financial situation. How much do you have currently? How much is your net worth growing each year as a percent? =FV(rate,nper,pmt,[pv],[type])

Is the resulting number inspiring or discouraging? Now what percent growth rate do you need to reach to make that number meaningful to your life plans? That might be a good target for your net worth growth. The growth goal is just for you, and it's not a contest. But you better believe that it's important. Goals create motivation, and the psychology works. The added benefit is that with a growth goal, you can now forecast your future. And once you buy into that future vision and know the growth number you need to get there, you'll have more than enough motivation to make it happen.

Your target growth rate could be dramatically different depending on where you are in your life and your income. There's no perfect target. And you should always be adjusting and reevaluating your goals. Regardless of the situation and circumstances, though, make those goals lofty. Don't listen to anyone who provides you a target without knowing your situation and your plans. Continue to make each month and each year better than that one before it. You might see a net worth decline in periods of unforeseen expense or during a recession, so use those periods to adjust and keep moving forward.

Remember This:

- *For the majority of your working life, simply focusing on net worth growth will be the best approach.*
- *Once you determine a specific plan for your life and your retirement, you can focus your attention on specific areas.*
- *Create annual goals as a percentage of growth.*
- *Evaluate the dollar amount you are growing relative to your spending to determine if you are growing enough.*

31. Tracking expenses and analysis

Once you know how much you have and how much you want to grow it, it's time to figure out how much you spend. You'll never know how long your money will last if you don't understand the run-rate. And when you understand it, you can improve upon it. But we're not just talking about measurement of expenses because discipline also plays a vital role in this exercise. You need to bring yourself closer to your expenses. There are many websites that will aggregate your credit card and bank account transactions, but it's not the same as doing it yourself. If an expense tracking solution is easy or convenient, that means it's easy for your brain to process and that's the exact opposite of what you need when you're starting this

Putting It Into Action

process. If you want to change your relationship with money, you need to be close to it.

You'll need to leverage your Excel skills again. For every single purchase you make, you will need an entry. Record the day and the amount, but also primary and secondary categories, along with the place of purchase. For example:

January 1: $25, Dining, Lunch, Chipotle

Date	Expense	Primary	Secondary	Vendor
1-Jan	$25	Dining	Lunch	Chipotle

Having this level of detail will allow you to analyze your spending in different ways:

- How is my spending different month-to-month? (Date Field)
- How much do I spend on eating out? (Primary Category Field)
- Do I spend more on dinners or lunches out? (Secondary Category Field)
- What restaurants do I spend the most? (Vendor Field)

Here are the primary and secondary categories I recommend and keep in mind that a trip to Target could be multiple categories; for those, create multiple entries for the one trip:

- Mortgage: Principal, Interest, Taxes
- Childcare: Each Child
- Medical: Each Person
- Groceries: NA

- Utilities: Gas, Power, Water, TV, Internet, Cell Phone
- Travel: Airfare, Hotel, Activities
- Lawn and Property Maintenance: Lawn Mowing, Leaf Blowing, Gardening
- Hobbies: Each Hobby or Each Person
- Personal Care: Gym/Activity Memberships, Hygiene/Beauty Products
- Dining: Breakfast, Lunch, Dinner, Drinks, Snacks, Alcohol
- Car: Repairs, Gas
- Entertainment: Whatever types you consume
- Clothing: Each Person
- Home Improvement: Materials, Services, Repairs
- Insurance: Car, Home, Anything else

There are several ways to tabulate these numbers and make them useable. I recommend pivot tables, but that's more on the advanced side of Excel. Simply "filtering" and summing totals for categories will also suffice. You're not going to need any regression analysis or advanced calculus here. Here is an example of how to track categories from month to month:

	January	February	March
Groceries	$604	$721	$589
Utilities	$492	$454	$501
Dining	$354	$389	$641
Entertainment	$174	$286	$103
Gas	$51	$42	$66

Putting It Into Action

The value of this exercise, in addition to the long-term planning uses, is to do it simply. If it takes you two hours every month to go through your receipts, that might be an indication that you're spending a bit too much. The power of tracking your spending is to become intimately familiar with your behavior and to begin to recognize trends and opportunities:

- Why is your electrical bill $225 every month?
- Wait, why is it now $250?
- What can I be doing regularly to lower that cost?
- What value do I really get for my $175 TV package?
- How did I spend $800 on groceries this month?
- And why was I charged twice for the same doctor's visit?

These are the types of questions you can't avoid asking when you start the (somewhat tedious and painful) task of tracking every cent you spend. There are easy ways to do this, but it is not the same as doing it yourself. There will come a time when you can tell yourself honestly that the discipline is no longer needed. But it won't be right this moment. No matter how good you think you are at being frugal or how well you think you understand your spending, you owe it to yourself to try this manual process for one month.

After you've done your first month's tracking, take a long, hard look, and ask if it was all worth it. I'm confident that you're spending considerably more than you think. And that you're not receiving value and a level of satisfaction commensurate with that spend. Each month you'll find opportunities to save, and you'll see the results almost immediately. Your spending sheet and your net worth chart will start to show results, and you'll gain momentum. You might even enjoy it.

Remember This:

- *You'll never know how long your money will last if you don't understand the run-rate.*

- *For every expense, record the day and the amount, but also primary and secondary categories, along with the place of purchase.*

- *No matter how good you think you are at being frugal or how well you think you understand your spending, you owe it to yourself to try this manual process for one month.*

32. Spending priorities and passions

Taking money out of the equation for a moment, having hobbies, interests, and passions makes for a rewarding and enjoyable life. Although my advice on the matter is less financial and relatively brief, the importance cannot be overstated. When you have hobbies and passions outside of your professional life, you have a buffer from many of the forces outside your control. You can't always control if your day at the office is enjoyable or painful, but you'll always have your personal activities. Those are within your control. There's no one holding you accountable to any measure of success unless your passion is competing against others, but even then it's your choice to compete.

So what are your core spending priorities? What are the things that you can and should spend money on to enrich your life and give you purpose? Pick a handful and feel free to change them over time (writing them in stone is not the purpose). I'd recommend health and education to start. Here are some more thought starters:

- What sort of entertainment do you enjoy most? Movies? Concerts? Theater?
- What sorts of hobbies satisfy you? Hiking? Gardening? Painting? Building model trains?
- What sorts of adventures broaden your view of the world? Camping? Cruising? Road trips?
- Who are the people who make you the happiest? Family? Friends? Like-minded strangers?
- What are the causes you believe in the most? Children? Poverty? Elderly? Environment?

If you don't know, that's OK. Actually, that's more than OK, that's tremendous. Because now one of your priorities can be to find your passion. Try it all. Travel everywhere. Build anything. Along the way, you'll stumble across the thing you enjoy the most, and you'll have it the rest of your life. And you will find something. The world is a big place, and there are a seemingly infinite number of activities, communities, and artistic expressions, forms of entertainment and sources of knowledge. You *will* find your passion.

Your New Relationship With Money

Once you have your list, write it down and make the conscious decision to not beat yourself up too much overspending in these areas. Here's the catch though, you need to figure out the minimum amount of money you need to pursue those priorities. Love to hike? You probably don't need $250 hiking boots every year. Have the travel bug? Skip the Business Class tickets and find a good deal. It's essential always to remember that this list is to alleviate guilt and maintain your focus, not as an excuse to spend freely.

The intention of this behavior to compartmentalize your passion spending as an independent category, one where you know absolutely that spending money translates directly into happiness. Depending on what your passions and priorities end up being, you might not need to spend money to participate in them, which is also good. But likely you'll need to spend money on these things, and you should *want* to do.

One last piece of advice: try to find a priority or two to share with your partner and your children. It will make for a happier life. And you'll save some money. Here's some space to make your list:

Remember This:

- *Hobbies and Passions make life more enjoyable.*
- *If you haven't found any yet, commit to discovering them.*
- *Make good spending decisions, but don't feel guilty about spending in your priority areas.*

Putting It Into Action

Core Spending Priority	Related Expenses
(Example) Health	• Organic fruits and vegetables, higher quality groceries. • Gym membership. • Good running shoes and bike. • Regular doctor visits.

33. Throw out your budgets

This one isn't so much an action-plan as it is an *inaction*-plan. The thing about budgets is that you'll always be just at it or slightly over it. And when you're over it, it's because you likely deemed the purchase to be worth the total expense; said another way, forgoing the expense would deprive you of some satisfaction or sustenance resulting in discomfort. It might be scandalous to say, but budgets aren't that useful when you're trying to improve your relationship with money. Budgets typically fall into two categories: Goals/Aspirations and Reminders.

Goals or Aspirational budgets would be a dramatic lifestyle change that you're not currently experiencing. For example, if you spend $1,000 a month on dinners out, an aspirational budget would be $200 a month. You're not even close. You'd have first to start saying no to friends, canceling your recurring date nights and skipping parties. You'd hit $900 in month one, $800 in month 2 and then find yourself more and more unhappy. There's little value in this progression. It's arbitrary and detrimental to your motivation.

Reminder budgets are when you take your paycheck, split it up into categories and then, based on your typical spending and savings goals, set reminders of where you need to be to stay on track. For example, if your grocery bills are generally between $500 and $600, a reminder budget is to stay at $550. The point of a reminder budget is not to forget what your targets are. They aren't dramatically aspirational. If you hit your reminder goal, you're happy about it, and you move on. If you don't, whatever. You don't strive for anything more.

The problem with these two typical budgets is that they don't address the core issue of your spending, which is finding your least expensive and ideal lifestyle. An aspirational budget moves the goal too fast making it difficult to attain and difficult to maintain after you reach it. A reminder budget doesn't change your mindset and only attempts to achieve consistency.

But Part 4 of this book is about action, so what should you do? You've set up your net worth chart, so you are now focused on growing, and you are currently tracking your spending, so you know where the opportunities are to cut costs. Your new view of budgeting should be that it's never good enough. This will take some discipline and time, but mainly, your "budgets" every week or month should be lower than they were the period before. Instead of saying, "I have $800 a month left for groceries and dining out, let's put $500 in groceries and $300 in dining," just throw that out the window and ask, "What's the minimum I can spend and still enjoy eating and being healthy?"

It's true that this is also a form of "budgeting" depending on your interpretation, but the main point I'd like to convey is that *conventional* budgeting isn't the answer. Conventional budgets are rigid, and you need actually to be flexible and agile. If we look at the groceries, the first step is to go and ask yourself for every item, "Do I need this?" and "Is there a cheaper alternative?" Let's take wine as an example because there won't be any health considerations in quality. Here's the decision path:

Your New Relationship With Money

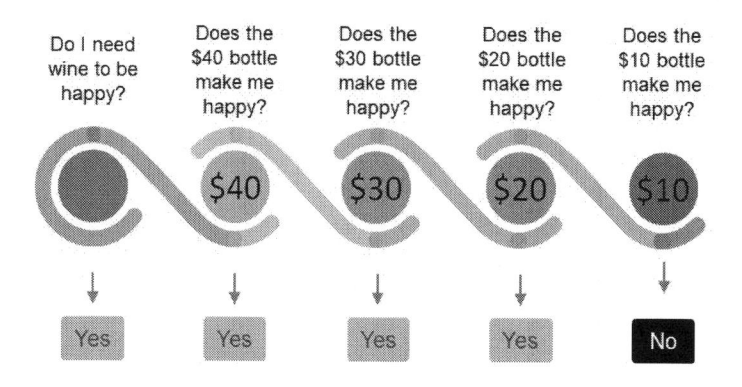

Do I need wine to be happy? → **Yes**
Does the $40 bottle make me happy? → **Yes**
Does the $30 bottle make me happy? → **Yes**
Does the $20 bottle make me happy? → **Yes**
Does the $10 bottle make me happy? → **No**

Now that you know where your limit is, insert an additional question:

Can I find the $20 bottle cheaper?
- Does the $20 bottle make me happy? → **Yes**
- Does the $10 bottle make me happy? → **No**
→ **Yes**

There you go. You've found your wine spending requirements. It might seem overwhelming to do this for everything you buy, but in most cases, it's easy and intuitive. It might take a few weeks or months to go through the decision tree, but eventually, you'll land on

Putting It Into Action

the ideal expense level. You'll probably also find that your recurring expenses aren't as numerous as you first think.

But what about more complicated purchases like a new deck for your house. A conventional budget would be to find out how much money you have available or can get in a home equity loan and that's your budget. And undoubtedly, you'll find a way to spend slightly more. The real question is, "How much is this deck worth *to me*?" And "is there an alternative I value more?" Here's the "budgeting" process for that:

1. What kind of deck would make me happy?
2. How much is that happiness worth? *$20,000*
3. Is the alternative (such as retiring a year earlier or going on a vacation) worth more? *No, the deck will provide more happiness.*
4. How much can I build that deck for? Quote A: *$35,000, B: $22,000, C: $15,000*

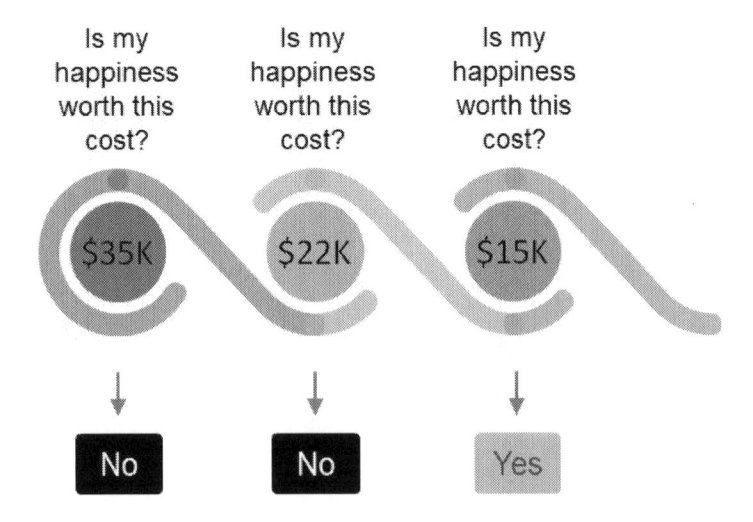

Is my happiness worth this cost?	Is my happiness worth this cost?	Is my happiness worth this cost?
$35K	$22K	$15K
No	No	Yes

5. For Quotes B and C, how much less happy will I be with C and how much more happy with B? *Unclear.*
6. Are the materials used in C of a quality that will create problems down the road, decreasing my happiness? *Yes.*

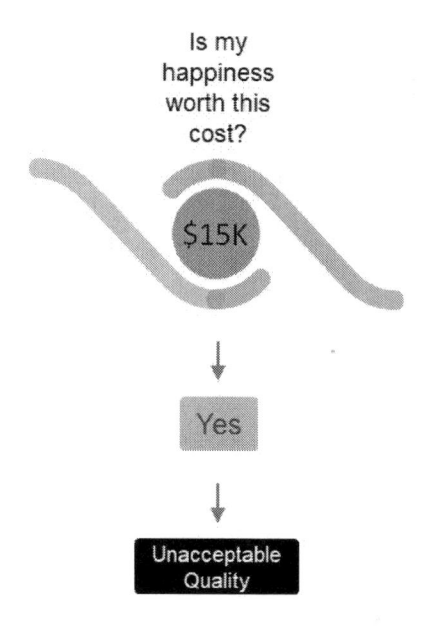

Is my happiness worth this cost?

$15K

↓

Yes

↓

Unacceptable Quality

7. For B, what can be done to lower the price? *Nothing.*
8. Reevaluate the 2nd bullet: Am I willing to forgo the deck for that additional $2,000, the difference between the quote of $22,000 and my happiness level of $20,000? *No.*

Putting It Into Action

Am I willing to forgo over this difference?

+$2K   −$5K

↓

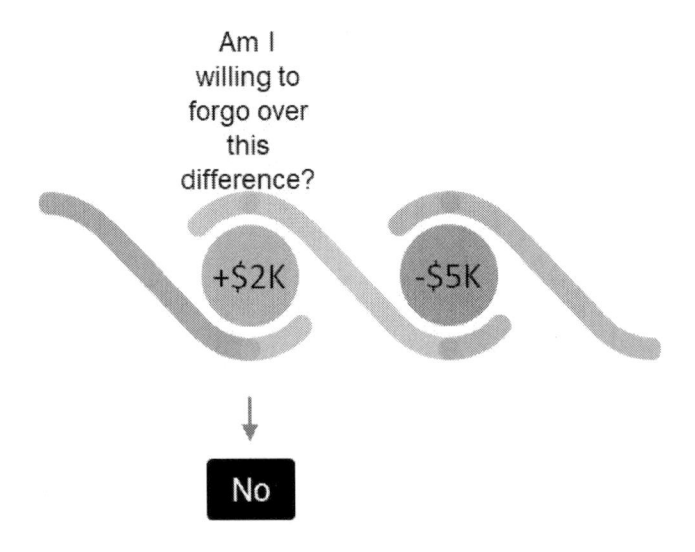

No

9. Build it with Option B at $22,000.

How is that any different than just setting a $20,000 budget? It's all about the decision tree. You may find that options exist for far less instead of just filling your budget because it's there to be filled. You might also decide not even to do it if the costs come back too high. Spending decisions aren't binary in that it's all or nothing. Spending decisions should be a series of choices, where the answer to one determines the following set of questions. Over time you'll grow accustomed to this process and eventually work your way through the decision tree intuitively. A $22,000 deck for your house or a $2.20 bottle of ketchup should have the same decision tree, although one will take you a little longer to think through.

So throw out your budgets and start evaluating the things you buy in terms of the happiness or functionality it gets you. Over time, perhaps very quickly, you'll narrow in on the right number for everything.

Remember This:

- *Your new view of budgeting should be that it's never good enough.*
- *Conventional budgets are rigid, and you need actually to be flexible and agile.*
- *For all your purchases, seek out cheaper and cheaper alternatives until you reach the point where you're no longer happy with it. The level right before that is where you should set your spending.*

34. Benefits at work

Remember Chapter 12 where everything is a trap and a way to separate you from your money? When it comes to benefits at work, take the opposite view: everything is a gift. A way to create more value in your life and keep you at that company. When it comes to compensation, especially if you are in a corporate job, your benefits can represent a substantial percentage of the overall package. Benefits can easily be equivalent to 20-30% of your base pay, so it's never something to take lightly or dismiss. On day one of a new job, print out the benefits documentation and study it carefully. It's worth your time.

At most large companies, there are many levels of the hierarchy and many titles. In general, though, large companies, especially publicly traded companies, are split into four primary tiers of employee type. Keep in mind that each of these tiers could have a handful of levels within them:

1. Non-Management
2. Management
3. Middle-Management
4. Officers/Executives

Why these 4 and not 3, combining Management and Middle Management? The difference is in the compensation structure: hourly vs. salaried, stock vs. cash, etc. So the four typical tiers are distinguished like this:

- Non-Management: Hourly employees, possibly unionized.
- Management: Salaried employees, cash bonus plans.
- Middle-Management: Salaried employees, stock bonus plans, optional structured compensation/benefits.
- Officers/Executives: Salaried employees, primarily stock-based compensation based on performance, large-scale stock incentives, optional structured compensation/benefits.

Even if you don't understand the programs that are available to you, if it's offered, there's a good chance that it's worth your time. And if it's a program that's made available to you only at a certain level, it must be a good thing and cost the company a lot; otherwise the company would give it to everyone.

There are a handful of categories that most employers provide benefits for:

Your New Relationship With Money

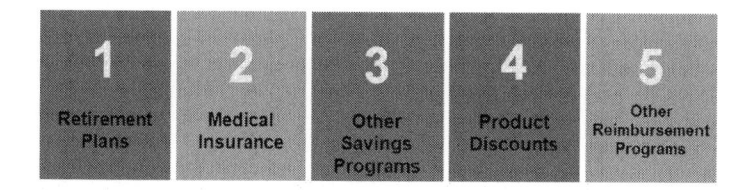

1	2	3	4	5
Retirement Plans	Medical Insurance	Other Savings Programs	Product Discounts	Other Reimbursement Programs

Although this book talks about retirement plans quite a bit, we'll still talk about those plans as it relates to evaluating your company's benefits:

1. Retirement Plans

While a 401k plan is standard these days, don't overlook the fine print and additional details from your employer. The percentage match on your contributions will vary between companies as will the vesting period, the time before the money becomes yours. In addition to 401ks, however, there might be after-tax 401ks, or Roth 401ks, which all provide slightly different benefits. Depending on your situation and life-planning, you might be able to leverage these nuanced options to great effect.

Although not typically available at most companies or to most employees, the real value of company-sponsored retirement plans are found in deferred compensation programs. These programs allow you to delay receiving income to avoid paying your current tax rate, which in theory is higher than at a future date you want to start receiving the money. If you are lucky enough to have one, max it out! As you can imagine, even Executives need to save for retirement, and most people start focusing on that near the ends of their careers. The savings programs available at many large companies are designed for those employees close to retirement so that the company can ensure that the employee is taken care of and can create an effective retirement plan (and leave on their own terms). If a program is designed to get a 60-year-old ramped up for retirement, imagine the impact it can have on someone 10, 20 or 30 years from retirement.

The programs are simple in design but can have several intricate details you'll have to work through, but mostly, you "defer" money from your paycheck to a future date. The primary benefit is that you don't pay income tax, which can be quite high if you are in your prime earning years. Like a 401k, the money grows via investments pre-tax, then you can receive the money at a pre-determined time or over a predetermined period. These are powerful earning tools and powerful planning tools. Do not pass them up.

2. Medical Insurance

Most people understand how medical insurance works, but having that benefit through work is probably not what you think it is. You can buy insurance yourself from the same providers with similar benefits and coverage. What a company-sponsored plan does is two-fold: first, the company reduces the cost by using its scale to negotiate better rates. They also then pay a portion of your monthly premium to lower your cost. If an insurance plan on the open market is $1,000 a month and has a $10,000 deductible, for example, a company would negotiate that down to $900 a month and a $9,000 deductible. And then they'd provide the plan to its employees for $500 a month and a $7,000 deductible. The difference between the open-market cost and what you pay is a value you should be aware of. It is typically substantial and probably the highest value of all your benefits.

Additionally, an open-market purchase of insurance isn't guaranteed to be upheld by the provider. They can change your rates or simply drop your coverage. This can be quite devastating for people who require medical care, so when an employer ensures that all its employees are covered, that's a big deal. Now, this isn't to say that the employer won't cancel its benefits program, but that's unusual.

While the value is most impactful for medical insurance, all insurance programs provided by an employer have the same built-in cost reductions: dental, vision, life, long-term disability, etc. Be sure to evaluate all your options.

3. Other Savings Programs

Any benefit listed in the "other" section probably doesn't garner much attention, but they can add up. Purchasing stock at a discount, Dependent Care FSAs and Health Savings Accounts, for example, can provide a few hundred to a few thousand dollars of value annually to those who participate. Do not underestimate the importance of stacking these opportunities together. Maybe your stock purchase program is limited to only a few hundred dollars a year; it is still worth your time. Over a career, a few hundred or a few thousand add up.

4. Product Discounts and Other Reimbursement Programs

By the time you've read through the 401k and Medical Insurance details, the final section of your benefits information won't keep your attention, but it should. Depending on what your company sells and where it's located, there could be a host of opportunities for you to save money. Discounts on the products it sells, for example, is a big one. If you are looking to join that company or leave that company, factor in this value when making that decision. It could very well add thousands of dollars to your overall compensation story. Working for an airline and getting free flights might be worth nothing to someone who never travels, but could be worth tens of thousands of dollars to a jet-setting family exploring the world.

Also, look for programs such as continuing education or degree-seeking reimbursement. Not only is the company paying for you to learn at your day job, but they're also willing to pay for your college degree, that's generous. They might even have partnerships with local colleges and universities which can create even larger savings.

You might not be able to participate in every program that's offered, but you should still explore and understand what's available. Perhaps you can't afford to contribute to an HSA this year; you should still learn everything you can about your plan. It might include a company match you weren't expecting and that motivates you into making a personal change so that you can participate. There might also be benefits that you are not eligible for because of your level in the company. You might get promoted soon, or maybe the benefits at the next level are so valuable, you gain the inspiration to reach the next level of your career.

There is also benefit in understanding the landscape of benefits. The package of benefits made available to employees is a key strategic decision by the employer to recruit and retain talented people. Understanding how these packages compare is an insightful indicator of a company's culture and their competitiveness in the job market. Remember back to Chapter 26 on negotiating.

Participating in and then maximizing benefits at work can create substantial additional value to you. There is a reason these benefits are available, and it's not a scam. If you're not fully versed in what's available and how it works, you are likely leaving a lot of money on the table.

Remember This:

- *Treat employment benefits as extra income. Don't pass it up.*
- *When it comes to compensation, especially if you are in a corporate job, your benefits can represent a substantial percentage of the overall package.*
- *Study your benefits even if you can't or don't want to participate.*

35. Retention departments and switching

If you're like most people, your cable, internet, and other recurring bills are too high. Switching can be a hassle, so most of you probably stick with your current providers and just suffer through it. Your recurring expenses and subscriptions, however small, are slowly eating away at you. $50 a month might not seem bad, but what about $600 a year? Or $6,000 over the next decade? Is $6,000 worth some action on your part? To be fair, there are subscription expenses we need, such as utilities and cell phones. Others you probably don't need as much, and then there are the subscriptions you don't even know you have or barely use. No matter the degree of necessity to your life, you can find savings in almost everything you pay for monthly.

Now that you're tracking your spending, it should become clear where your money is going every month. Hopefully, some of these entries will be a painful wake-up call to your spending. It isn't a coincidence that your recurring expenses and subscriptions seem innocuous and acceptable when you stumble across the bill from time to time. There are teams of marketers making sure you spend as much as possible without causing you to drop the service. You're the victim here, so don't feel too bad. Feel a little bad, though. Just bad enough to do something about it.

I recommend that you evaluate all the companies you pay a monthly bill to on an annual basis. Every year you should ask yourself the following questions:

1. Do I still need this?
2. Is there a cheaper alternative within the same provider?
3. Is there a cheaper competitor?
4. What is the minimum price I can get this for?

Current providers want you to stay, and competitors want you to switch. Both groups will, therefore, make it appealing to do what they want, and that's where you can find the benefit. Service providers need you more than you need them. Make everyone work a little bit harder to keep your business. If a quick phone call can save you $20 a month, that's $240 a year and $2,400 over the next ten years. And that is a pretty significant savings rate for the amount of time you put in. Don't tell yourself that $20 isn't worth your time, because it's not $20. It's $2,400.

Almost every company will have some sort of retention department or program, aimed at retaining you as a customer. When you call your TV provider, what options do you hear? Probably:

- To pay your bill, press one.
- To set up new service, press two.
- To report a technical problem, press three.
- To cancel service, press four.

Number four is the retention department. They are measured on how many customers they interact with that <u>don't</u> cancel service. They succeed when you get enough additional value to reconsider your desire to cancel. They want to give you a special offer. They want to make it work for you. Don't be afraid to press four and speak to someone in the retention department.

You may not be able to get a discount, that's certainly a possibility. But you'll probably find one. There's just too much competition for a provider to lose you as a customer. Don't be tricked by any offer that isn't a discount though. If you call to cancel your TV service and they offer you free HBO, you're not saving money. In fact, you're probably getting tricked again because in three or six months that HBO will be gone and you'll either have a higher monthly bill or be back where you started. You want money. Don't let them off the hook.

Additionally, be wary of contracts. If you choose to switch or are offered a discount involving a contract, analyze it

Putting It Into Action

carefully. It's probably not in your best interest. Consider two rules for evaluating contracts on monthly services:

1. Never sign a contract for more than 12 months. Very rarely does a provider give you the value you're expecting. 2, 3, or 4-year contracts are not for your benefit; keep that in mind.
2. After the contract ends, call your provider and say you want to cancel.

You might feel a little awkward challenging a representative about cost or requesting a discount, but you shouldn't. The person across the counter or over the phone doesn't care one bit. They do this all day, every day and it's no money out of their pocket. Their feelings aren't hurt if you leave either.

If the thought of being disloyal pops into your head during this process, shake it away. Companies are not loyal to customers in the interpersonal sense of the word. Companies only do what helps them grow profits, and sometimes, those actions and behaviors *look* like loyalty, but they're most certainly not. The best description of these behaviors is "consistent" or "proactive," but not "loyal." Even if you do believe a company is loyal to you, the only real test is to ask them for something that hurts them and benefits you. Put them to the test. You may save some money.

Remember This:

- *Your recurring expenses and subscriptions, however small, are slowly eating away at you.*
- *Make everyone work a little bit harder to keep your business by calling the retention department and asking for a discount.*
- *If a quick phone call can save you $20 a month, that's $240 a year and $2,400 over the next ten years.*

36. Saving money vs. not spending money

The simple truth and this is quite obvious, is that saving money means not spending it. There are ways to spend more efficiently, that's true, but not buying something at all is the most powerful thing you can do. My sister used to annoy our Dad with news of "sales" and "deals" when we were kids. "This dollhouse is 40% off, Dad! Look how much money we can save!" After a couple of years of this, our Dad replied, "I can't afford for you to keep saving me money." And it became a running joke in the family. But the lesson was practical: you're not saving money if something costs less than its normal price, whatever the retailer determines that to be. You're still spending it.

Saving money is not spending money on the dollhouse. Or the car. Or clothes. We talked about your priorities for spending in Chapters 7 and 32, and we talked about budgeting in Chapter 33; those are focused on spending money only to the level at which your happiness and satisfaction begin to decline. This chapter takes that a bit further. And it's tough. Hence putting this chapter later in the book to build up your tolerance to such ideas.

The first question you asked yourself about that bottle of wine in chapter 33 was, "Does this make me happy?" And in the scenario, the answer was yes. Let's ask a different question, "Would I be unhappy without wine at all?" When you first frame up the question if it makes you happy, chances are the answer is yes. We don't actively purchase things that make us *unhappy,* right? It's safe to say that if you're buying wine, it makes you happy. Everything shiny and new makes you happy. At least for a time. The challenge becomes to cut it out and see what happens.

As you go through your spending tracking and find areas to save money, you will undoubtedly find numerous opportunities to save 40% off the dollhouse. And that's great! I don't want you to think that those exercises aren't valuable. They are incredibly useful and also challenging to execute. You should feel delighted if you can get to that point. But it might not be enough to achieve your goals. And most likely it's not the best you can do. If you want to make dramatic changes in your finances, you're going to have to make dramatic lifestyle changes in your spending.

Let's work through this in manageable chunks. When it comes to not spending money, there are three buckets that your opportunities will fall into:

Your New Relationship With Money

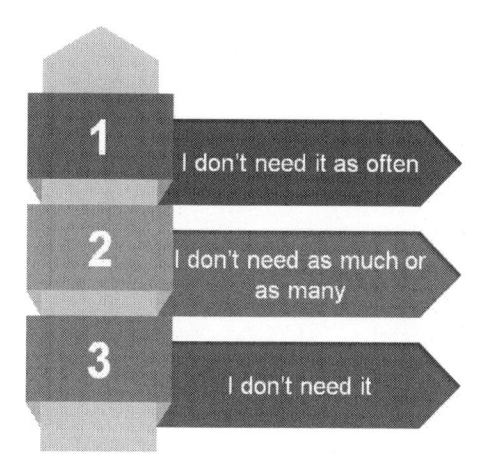

1. I don't need it as often
2. I don't need as much or as many
3. I don't need it

Remember, these are different than the earlier chapter on budgeting, which focuses on a 4th bucket: Can I find this cheaper. Some examples of spending that you can eliminate through reduction of frequency might be:

- Dining out
    - *Do I need to eat lunch out five days a week?*
- Entertainment
    - *Do I need to go to the movies every other week?*
- Self-Care
    - *Do I need to get my nails done once a month? (Note: I have no idea how frequently people do this.)*

In all of these examples, you are cutting out a purchase entirely. This is different than continuing to dine out five times a week, but look for specials or use coupons. As you can see, these examples are activities. So as you track your spending, sort all the activity-based spending and know where you can reduce your frequency of the events.

Putting It Into Action

So what about bucket number two? Here are some examples:

- Clothing
  - *Do I need to buy three pairs of jeans when one will do?*
- Food
  - *Do I need to order a dessert or an extra side with dinner?*
- Home Décor
  - *Do I need ten decorative candles for my living room?*

This category is about stuff and the quantity you buy. It's not about finding a great deal on jeans and buying three pairs; it's about buying fewer items. You can also find a deal on that one pair, but regardless, you're spending less money overall than with three pairs.

The last and most crucial bucket are those purchases you simply don't need. If we look at the example of food, it's good to find a deal on your meal out. It's better to reduce the amount of food you buy during those activities. Even better to go less frequently. The last steps are where you find the most savings, and that is not to buy it at all. If you want to save money, you have to stop spending it and that means a conscious decision to cut something out. Here are some thought starters:

- Do I need cable TV or can I live without all that HGTV?
- Do I need to get my nails done? (Note: Again, I have no idea how often this happens, how much it costs, or anything about it)
- Does my car need all these tune-ups or is the dealership just making this up?

- Do I need new shoes and does anyone even notice?
- Do I need early boarding on my flight, or will I be miserable no matter what?
- Does my living room need to be painted, or am I just bored?

Here is the metric by which you can track your success: total *number* of purchases. With your spending tracking in place, you can easily count how many times you buy something or pay for a service. If you have 50 purchases in month one and 40 in month two, you're on the right track. It might not be as significant at first; after all, you're probably making a lot of significant life changes simultaneously. But do keep an eye on not just your net worth and your total spending amount, but your number of purchases as well. It will make a huge difference.

If you describe saving money in conjunction with a purchase, I challenge you to change the way you view saving. When your neighbor buys a new car after two years, and you don't, that's saving. When your colleagues go out for lunch, and you don't, that's saving. There is a robust psychological draw toward spending money because it's instantly gratifying. Not spending it and not getting that gratification can sometimes have a negative impact. This will be challenging for many people to overcome. The first stage will be to recognize that you must change this behavior. You will overcome the negative feelings of missing out. Eventually, you may grow to enjoy your newfound discipline. At that point, you're a real saver.

Remember This:

- *Saving money means not spending it.*
- *To really jump-start your savings, find areas to cut out spending, not just be more efficient at spending.*
- *Track the number of expenses you have, not just the amount you spend. Try to reduce the number of times you pull out the credit card.*

37. Divvying up your paycheck

When cash is deposited into your checking account, it is in its least productive form. It feels good to get it there and ready to be spent, but getting cash means that you've either exhausted your tax benefits and employee benefits or that you've missed the opportunity. If we go back to the tax and retirement savings Chapters, 22 and 23 respectively, you'll remember that siphoning off chunks of your gross income into a 401k, for example, can not only save you on the taxes but get you a matching contribution from your employer. And that's just one tool. In addition to all the government savings programs, your employer probably has optional programs for you to participate, such as stock purchase plans or deferred income plans. Your goal should be to put your paycheck to work. Send that money to whatever destination gets you the greatest tax break, the highest match or the most significant return. Ideally, you'll want to work toward a point where you take home just enough to cover expenses and then put the rest automatically into other places. Funding your tax breaks and benefits should be your top priority, not your spending. It's ok not being able to fully max out your 401k at $19,000 a year and your HSA at $3,500 and so on, but that should be your goal before you consider how to spend the remaining cash.

While this list won't be comprehensive or entirely applicable to everyone, it should be a good representation of what options are available to most people who work for companies. If you work for a small business or some other entity which doesn't provide these options, it's not the end of the world. You'll miss the opportunity for certain tax breaks and benefits, but you'll have more cash to invest in taxable accounts, purchase real estate, pay down your mortgage, etc. Everyone will have opportunities to maximize their income. You need to go through the options available to you individually. Step one is to use your spend tracker to determine what is the absolute minimum amount of cash you need. This minimum includes your mortgage, gas for your car, groceries, basic utilities, etc. We'll say that this is $2,000 every two weeks for simplicity.

Here's where things get a little more complicated, and it will be up to you to understand the math of your specific paycheck's tax withholdings. For this exercise, we'll look at someone earning $100,000 annually and make some simplifying assumptions. If you do nothing in regards to paycheck deductions, you'll have $25,000 withheld for taxes (25%), and your annual takehome pay will be $75,000, which equates to $2,885 per paycheck, assuming 26 biweekly pay periods. Knowing your bare minimum

Putting It Into Action

expenses needs of $2,000, you'd have $885 left each period to repurpose into a savings tool. But that assumes there are no tax savings to be had first, which isn't the case.

Paycheck Components	$100,000 Salary
Bi-Weekly Paycheck	$3,846
Remaining After 25% Taxes	$2,885
Average Expenses	($2,000)
Remaining Cash	$885

Now it's time to start divvying up the money.

- **401k**
  - *You'll want to contribute the maximum that is matched, which is usually 6%. On $100,000 income, that's $6,000 annually, $231 per paycheck.*
- **Health Savings Account**
  - *There's typically no company match, but the IRS limit is $3,500 for individuals. That's $135 per paycheck.*

What you've now done is to reduce your taxable income. So instead of paying 25% on $100,000, you're paying 25% on $100,000 less $6,000 of the 401k and $3,500 of the HSA. Again, simplifying the scenario to illustrate the point. Your new taxable income is $90,500, you have $22,625 withheld in taxes instead of $25,000, and your take-home pay is $2,611; not such a big difference from the fully unutilized $2,885.

Paycheck Components	$100,000 Salary
Bi-Weekly Paycheck	$3,846
401k Contribution	($231)
HSA Contribution	($135)
Remaining After 25% Taxes	$2,611
Average Expenses	($2,000)
Remaining Cash	$611

You have some more decisions to make. You might decide that you need the $611 above your minimum spending to cover other expenses and that's ok. As your income grows or your expenses reduce, you will need that extra money in paycheck less and less. But for this example, let's assume that you already have cash on hand and you don't need that $611. Immediately after your decisions about the 401k and HSA, you should consider making Roth IRA contributions.

- **Roth IRA**
  - *The annual IRS limit is $6,000, which is $231 if you want to contribute every two weeks.*

Putting It Into Action

Remaining Cash	$611
Roth IRA Contribution	($231)
Remaining Cash	$380

Your new take home is $380. We can now revisit the 401k because although you contributed the max your company matches, you didn't max out the IRS limit.

- **401k Revisited**
  - *Your 6% contribution of $6,000 leaves $13,000 left before hitting the IRS max. That's $500 per paycheck.*

If you are now deducting $19,000 from your $100,000, your taxable income drops to $77,500. So mathematically, we are now adjusting the takehome pay because you are making an increased pre-tax contribution. You withhold $19,375 in taxes. Your take-home pay drops to $58,125 annual or $2,235 per paycheck, just enough to cover your Roth contributions. And you have $5 left. Here is how the math flows:

Your New Relationship With Money

Paycheck Components	$100,000 Salary
Bi-Weekly Paycheck	$3,846
401k Contribution	($731)
HSA Contribution	($135)
Remaining After 25% Taxes	$2,236
Average Expenses	($2,000)
Remaining Cash	$236
Roth IRA Contribution	($231)
Remaining Cash	$5

The challenging part of this exercise is that withholdings are not so simple, and neither are your expenses. It will take some time for you to find the sweet spot in your paycheck deductions. The objective is to make your money work, maximize your opportunities, and then live with the rest. If you wait for the opportunity where your spending allows you to save, you'll never find it. In the example above, you'd tell yourself that you earn $100,000 a year, feeling pretty good about yourself, and start making spending decisions based on that number. But you earn $75,000 because you owe taxes and that doesn't afford you the same opportunities. The more disciplined approach is to maximize your savings tools and then tell yourself that you make whatever is left over after you've taken advantage of your savings opportunities.

If you can find that mindset and learn to live with it as the reality, you'll be growing your net worth substantially and changing the trajectory of your life.

Remember This:

- *When cash is deposited into your checking account, it is in its least productive form.*
- *If you wait for the opportunity where your spending allows you to save, you'll never find it.*
- *Send your paycheck money to whatever destination gets you the greatest tax break, the highest match, or the most significant return.*

38. Start investing yesterday

I've spent a lot of time talking about investments, compounding growth and retirement accounts, but you're probably asking, "How *exactly* do I do that?!" This chapter will be about the mechanics of investing in the stock market. While there are many companies through which you can manage investments, I will show examples from Charles Schwab because I find their interfaces to be the most intuitive and their resources the most robust.

Your New Relationship With Money

Prepare yourself for a short chapter, because this is all relatively easy.

To open a brokerage account, visit the website, in this case www.schwab.com, and navigate to opening a brokerage account. The form is online and simple.

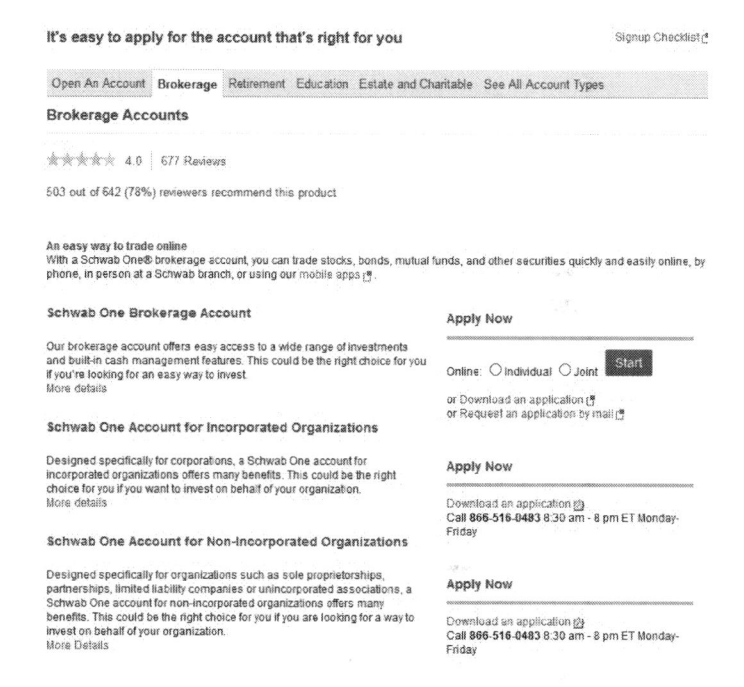

Jumping ahead to your open account, you'll be provided instructions for funding it via check or bank transfer. Move the money you want to start investing into this account. Once the funds are there, you can start trading.

Putting It Into Action

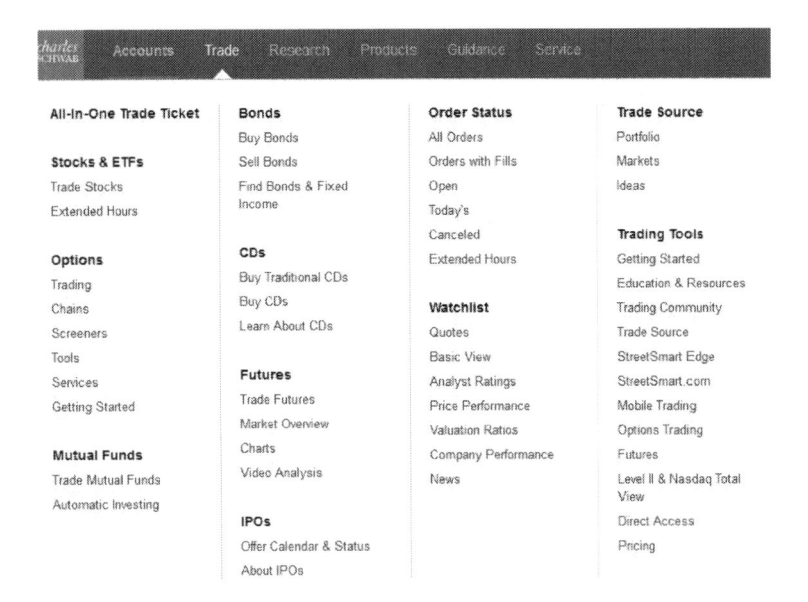

Under "Trade," find Stocks and ETFs, and select trade stocks. You'll be given this form to place your order. All brokerage accounts will have the same fields, so if you choose a different company, you'll still have to make the same selections.

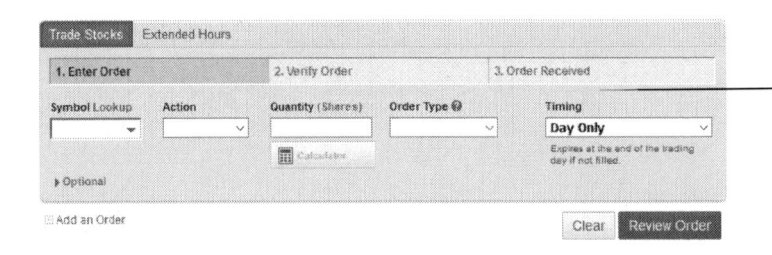

Now we can make our selections and place the order:

1. The symbol is the ticker for the stock or ETF. In the example below, I've entered Apple: AAPL.
2. The action you want to take is either Buy or Sell.

3. Enter the number of shares you want to buy or sell next.
4. Order type can be confusing, so until you've gotten comfortable with investing, only select Market Order, which means the order will be executed at whatever the market price is at that second.
5. Timing should be Day Only which means that if the order expires at the end of the day if it doesn't execute. Don't worry about that one.
6. Always, always, always select the box for Reinvest Dividends. Always.

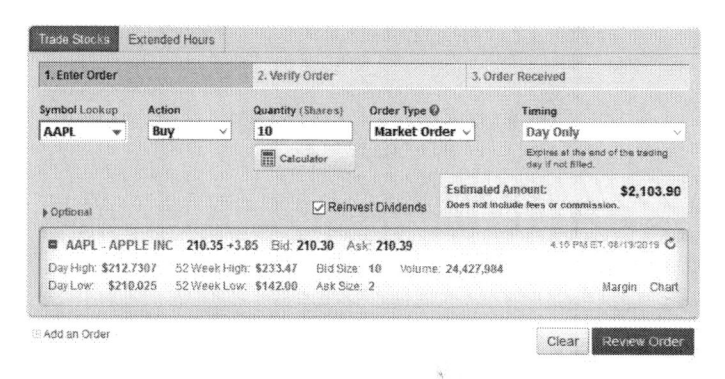

In this example, you'll be buying ten shares of Apple and reinvesting the dividends. The total value for this is $2,103.90. You'll pay your commission, which is usually $5-10 and the order will be placed.

It's all very easy. And you can always call the brokerage firm and place an order over the phone too. They want to make it easy for you to invest. If you're nervous about the process, do a couple of practice runs. Log in to your accounts and start digging around. Check out the research sections, read the reports, scrutinize their portfolio recommendations and just get comfortable with the pages. You'll quickly grow accustomed to making transactions quickly and efficiently.

Remember This:

- *Buying and selling stocks, ETFs and Mutual Funds is easy.*
- *Go sign up for a brokerage account if you don't already have one.*

39. Annual lifestyle deflation

If you've ever taken it upon yourself to do some spring cleaning, empty the attic or go through your old files, you've undoubtedly asked yourself, "How is this still here?!" Your finances are similar in that money comes and go, expenses come and go, investments, accounts, assets, etc. When you go through your finances and expenses for the first time and set up your various charts, hopefully, you've taken the opportunity to clean house. This can't be a one-time event, though.

In previous chapters, we've covered the thought-processes for evaluating your spending and your investments, and while the process won't change, your priorities, your needs, and of course market conditions will drive different decisions. Therefore, the choices you made at age 20 or 30 or 40 might not apply five years later.

Your New Relationship With Money

I would even argue they may not apply five months later. The world changes as does your life, so you must be evaluating your spending regularly. At the very least, make a point of creating a new baseline every year.

There are two categories that people rarely deflate in spending; voluntarily deflate, I should say. Convenience and Luxury are the areas of lifestyle and spending that seem to grow the most consistently and never revert. If your first car is a 15-year-old Honda Accord and your next car is a new Honda Accord, followed by a Nissan Maxima and then a BMW 5 Series, you don't see many people going back to the used Accord. That same pattern applies to convenience. Few people outsource tasks like yard work only to do it themselves ten years later. But if you are to make improvements in your financial life, you must deflate certain areas of your life when the level of spending exceeds its most efficient return.

As I discussed in Chapter 11 on lifestyle inflation, there is certainly benefit and happiness to be found in certain categories of inflation. There are also certain temporary situations in life where some inflation is the best use of your money. Buying a house to raise a family might be the best decision you ever make, but when your kids move out, you might not find the same happiness and utility from the extra bedrooms, backyard, and neighborhood. Lifestyle deflation would be to move to a smaller home or apartment. But if you trade size for luxury and buy a new place at the same cost, you've saved nothing. You've freed up nothing to pursue the latest activities or financial needs in your life.

This deflation can and should be done regularly. It can be as simple as the groceries you buy, the clothes you wear and the entertainment you enjoy. Perhaps you love going to concerts and over time as your income has increased, your seats get closer and closer to the stage; the cost rises exponentially. It will be tough for you to start then moving backward to save money, but this isn't punishment. The point is that you are different than you were then. The concerts are different and the crowds different. Moving one section back might not hinder your enjoyment of the concert. You may prefer sitting in a different place. If you don't deliberately look for this type of deflation opportunity though, you'll never see these choices as anything other than punishment.

Travel can be another area where deflation never crosses your mind. When you're in college, and you travel, you'll sleep on a friend's couch. When you start to make money, that couch becomes a cheap hotel. And then a nicer hotel. And a slightly nicer one. From $100 a night to vacations where you simply can't comprehend staying in anything less than $1,000 a night. You might even filter out hotels less than a $1,000 in your searches because that level of lodging is the new normal. In reality, though, $900 hotels and $800 hotels and $500 hotels are all the same. Taking a step back to normalize and deflate your lifestyle will save you a lot of money and won't ruin your vacation. You'll have more money for other activities or to travel longer.

Finding areas of opportunity to save money is a lifelong exercise. You can control your lifestyle inflation to a degree, and that takes discipline, but merely slowing the rate of inflation won't be enough because there will be extenuating circumstances outside your control or that you decide are worth the inflation. Revaluating your level of spending regularly isn't punishment and doesn't detract from the joy you had in "earning" something before. Perhaps you'll find it enjoyable. It's important to remember that you and your life and constantly changing. It's ok to reflect and determine that you no longer need to do things the same way.

Remember This:

- *Spring clean your finances every year to find areas to reduce spending.*
- *What was "worth it" and normal before might not be needed anymore.*
- *Slowing the rate of lifestyle inflation isn't enough. You need to actively find areas to deflate categories of spending.*

40. Financial independence

Your relationship with money is going to change over time as it serves different purposes at different times in your life. For the latter part of your life, your relationship with money will ideally be one where you no longer need to earn it. At that point, money serves solely to facilitate your self-actualization, the top of Maslow's Hierarchy. The point where your relationship with money is how to spend it, no longer how to earn it is the point of financial independence.

In the first part of this book, I explained that there's no standard path you can follow to financial betterment or independence. It's challenging to find the path within the forest, and forces are trying to pull you off course the entire time. Therefore, it is somewhat of an impossible task to explain precisely how you can become financially independent. Anyone promising the silver bullet to do so is at best generalizing and most likely leading you astray. Truly, only you can figure out how you can make this all happen. You can do it, though! If you can change the way you think about money, develop the skills and tools necessary to make improvements and stick with it, you can become financially independent. It might not be as soon as you like, but you can do it.

All that being said, I'd like to introduce you to a concept I call the Backward Income Method. In a nutshell, you work your way from your approximate death (morbid, I know), estimating your spending needs and your available income at that time. Once you go down in age and reach the point where your money runs out, that's your financial independence date.

Before we get into the easy math, let's talk about income. Income comes in three primary forms:

1. Defined Payments
2. Asset-Based Distributions
3. Asset Conversion

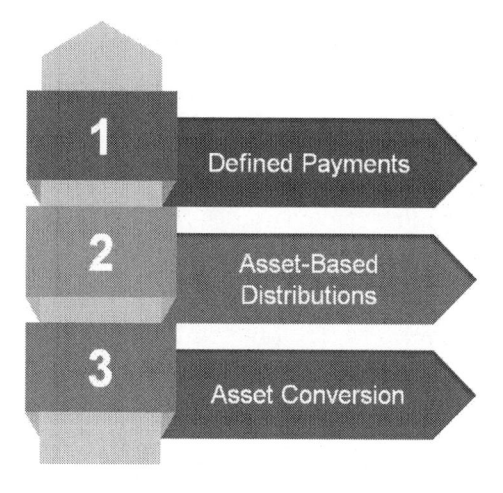

The first is probably the most well-known. Social Security and other pension or annuity-type programs are defined payments. You get a defined amount of money each period, and maybe it increases over time, but it's clearly defined. There is no underlying asset you can sell like a house. If you die, the payments go away (unless you've chosen to have spousal benefits, but we'll skip that part in this chapter) and there's no residual value at that point.

Asset-based distributions and asset conversion overlap a bit in that they can share the same source: an investment asset. The two most common types of distributions are rents and dividends. For the first example, the asset is a house, and the distribution is the rent payment. The second example is a stock that pays a quarterly dividend. In both of these, the asset has a value, which can change depending on several factors. You can sell the asset at any time. But if you hold it, someone is paying you for that. A company is paying you a dividend, or a tenant is paying you to live in it. You can continue receiving these

Putting It Into Action

payments for as long as you want and then sell the asset if you choose.

Asset conversion is just spending money you are converting from a different type of investment. Or also just spending down your savings. If you sell $100,000 of stock and then spend it, that's asset conversion. Or if you sell that rental property and spend the resulting cash, that's also a conversion. The big difference between the conversion of an asset and the distribution from an asset is that once you sell an asset, it can't grow, and it also can't create income. Take the house for example: If it's worth $300,000 and generates $1,000 a month in rent, if you keep it for ten years, the house might be worth $400,000, and you will have also collected 120 rent payments. But if you sell it at the starting point, you get $300,000, and that's it.

Let's take an easy example. You are 40 years old and have $50,000 in a 401K and you stop making contributions. We'll ignore Social Security for now. You anticipate that you'll live until 90 and need $100,000 a year pre-tax. The rough math at 5% growth each year means that at age 86, you'll have around $471,000. If you withdraw $100,000 a year and the remainder continues to grow, you'll run out around at age 90. And then die. Again, sorry to be morbid.

In this example, $50,000 is worth five years of financial independence later in life. If you have $100,000, then instead of age 86, you can stop working earlier. What about $200,000? What if you only need $50,000 a year for expenses instead of $100,000? Things get interesting when your assets grow and/or, or you accrue them at earlier ages, and your expenses decrease.

Your New Relationship With Money

The first step is to plot out your expenses for the rest of your life, by factoring in things like travel, college tuition for your kids, new cars, medical expenses and all the possible things that could pop up. Make sure to account for inflation, so if you spend $500 a month on groceries today, 30 years from now, you'll most certainly be paying more for the same stuff. This is a tough exercise for sure. Do the best you can, but stay on the conservative side.

For simplicity, let's assume you are 40 years old and expect a flat $100,000 a year in expenses for your life.

Step 1: Estimate your Social Security

- Expect to start taking Social Security around age 70. Let's say that it's $2,000 for you and $2,000 for your spouse.
- That's $4,000 a month. $48,000 a year.

Step 2: Estimate other defined benefits like Pensions

- If you have a pension or another defined annuity-style program, you'll likely have tools available to estimate payments at different times. Let's say that you start taking those payments at age 65.
- That's $2,000 a month. $24,000 a year.

If you're keeping track, you have $24,000 a year from age 65 until 90 and $48,000 from age 70 to 90. That's $72,000 a year from age 70 to 90. That won't be enough from age 70 on, because you're $28,000 short annually. And you're $76,000 short at age 65.

Building this out in Excel, with each five-year period a column, you can see how this takes shape. With the initial

Putting It Into Action

income sources below you can't retire on Social Security and Pension alone, which you can see by the negative numbers in the "net" row.

Age	40	45	50	55	60	65	70	75	80	85	90
Social Security							$48K	$48K	$48K	$48K	$48K
Pension						$24K	$24K	$24K	$24K	$24K	$24K
Total Pre-Tax Income	$0K	$0K	$0K	$0K	$0K	$24K	$72K	$72K	$72K	$72K	$72K
Expenses	($100K)	($100K)	($100K)	($100K)	($100K)	($100K)	($100K)	($100K)	($100K)	($100K)	($100K)
Net	($100K)	($100K)	($100K)	($100K)	($100K)	($76K)	($28K)	($28K)	($28K)	($28K)	($28K)

Let's keep building it up:

Step 3: Estimate your Asset-Based Distributions

- You have a rental property which generates $1,000 a month. $12,000 a year. We'll assume rent stays flat.
- You have $300,000 in your 401k growing at 6% annually, and you start withdrawing at age 60 at which point it will be worth $962,000.
  - ➢ *Assume that switch to more conservative investments earning 4% and you can safely withdraw 4% of this balance each year and not deplete the principal amount. This is $38,500 annually.*

Age	40	45	50	55	60	65	70	75	80	85	90
Social Security							$48K	$48K	$48K	$48K	$48K
Pension						$24K	$24K	$24K	$24K	$24K	$24K
Rental Income	$12K	$12K	$12K	$12K	$12K	$12K	$12K	$12K	$12K	$12K	$12K
401k					$39K	$39K	$39K	$39K	$39K	$39K	$39K
Total Pre-Tax Income	$12K	$12K	$12K	$12K	$51K	$75K	$123K	$123K	$123K	$123K	$123K
Expenses	($100K)	($100K)	($100K)	($100K)	($100K)	($100K)	($100K)	($100K)	($100K)	($100K)	($100K)
Net	($88K)	($88K)	($88K)	($88K)	($50K)	($26K)	$23K	$23K	$23K	$23K	$23K

You now have enough to retire at 70, and you're getting close at 65, and you're a ways away from stopping work at age 60. Again, look at the net row on the bottom to see when the negative numbers turn positive.

Your New Relationship With Money

Step 3 Continued: Estimate your Asset-Based Distributions

- You have $200,000 in dividend-paying stocks paying 5% annually.

You can use this non-retirement asset to fill the gap between the time you want to retire and when you're eligible for your retirement accounts and can afford to stop. You keep reinvesting the dividends until age 55, at which point you have $416,000, assuming the underlying share price stays flat. You start withdrawing the investment by $50,000.

Age	40	45	50	55	60	65	70	75	80	85	90
Social Security							$48K	$48K	$48K	$48K	$48K
Pension							$24K	$24K	$24K	$24K	$24K
Rental Income	$12K	$12K	$12K	$12K	$12K	$12K	$12K	$12K	$12K	$12K	$12K
401k						$39K	$39K	$39K	$39K	$39K	$39K
Investments					$50K	$50K					
Total Pre-Tax Income	$12K	$12K	$12K	$12K	$101K	$125K	$123K	$123K	$123K	$123K	$123K
Expenses	($100K)	($100K)	($100K)	($100K)	($100K)	($100K)	($100K)	($100K)	($100K)	($100K)	($100K)
Net	($88K)	($88K)	($88K)	($88K)	$1K	$25K	$23K	$23K	$23K	$23K	$23K

With your extra non-retirement savings, you can fill the expense gap from age 60 to 70 and stop working. And you'll still have about $250,000 leftover. And don't forget about that 401k balance that you're only withdrawing 4% from; that principal will continue to hold its value assuming the investment continues its growth. You'll want to be conservative in this exercise and holding onto a buffer or safety net such as the $250,000, or the 401k balance is essential. You don't know what your expenses will be like in the future or how much help you'll want to provide to your children. One thing is for certain though: you won't be able to return to work and earn what you used to. Unless you are a celebrity CEO that is.

The example we walked through is overly simplified, and there will be many more elements of your life and future that need to be accounted for. Being conservative is a good thing, but being too conservative means you'll be working longer than you have to, and you'll find yourself with much more money than you can spend.

You might be looking at these tables and thinking, "financial independence looks impossible." Depending on your circumstances, it might be tough to attain, even at 70. Or maybe you could get there by 40. Only when you develop an intimate knowledge of your income, expenses, and assets can you determine what's realistic. And if you do those things and your timeline to reach financial independence is ten years too late, you have to ask yourself, "what sacrifices am I willing to make?"

Financial Independence doesn't mean you need to stop working. It doesn't mean that you wear khakis and walk along the beach. It's going to be completely different for everyone. At what age you reach it, how much you spend, what you do, where you live. Financial independence can look like whatever you want it to look like. That's why it's called *independence,* right? The one constant is that it requires money. It also takes some degree of sacrifice. Your relationship with money, and with spending are going to be lifelong balancing acts. You will also have to strengthen your relationship with inconvenience and discipline. Your relationship with money will also impact your real-life relationships, likely for the better.

If you want to achieve your purpose, you'll need financial independence. And this will take time. I recommend starting right now.

Your New Relationship With Money

I chose to use the word relationship to title this book because there's no equation, rule, or silver bullet for being rich and being happy. Like relationships with people, relationships with money, how you feel about it, how you treat it, what you do for it, can be complicated. It can create a lifetime of difficulty. There's no easy fix to this. So in the same way that interpersonal relationships are built over time, built on compromise and understanding, so too is your relationship with money.

I hope that this book has changed your perspective and you've grown your knowledge, not with the expectation that you're now an expert, but with a framework by which you change the way money comes and goes in your life. Now is the time to start a new relationship with money or improve the one you had.

Relationships are hard. Really hard. But when you find the right ones, they enrich your life and give it meaning. Money is no different. I hope you will forever enjoy your new relationship with money.

Your Notes

Your Notes

Your Notes

Your Notes

Your Notes

Your Notes

Made in the USA
Monee, IL
21 September 2020